Tales

of the Heartily Homeschooled

Little Dozen Press
Ontario, Canada

Tales of the Heartily Homeschooled

Published by Little Dozen Press
Windsor, Ontario, Canada
http://www.littledozen.com

Copyright 2008
by Rachel Starr Thomson and Carolyn Joy Currey

Visit the authors at http://rachelstarrthomson.blogspot.com

Cover artwork and design by Deborah Thomson
Copyright 2008

All rights reserved. No part of this publication may be reproduced, stored in a retrieval system, or transmitted, to any form or by any means, electronic, mechanical, photocopying, recording, or otherwise, without the prior written permission of the publisher.

ISBN: 978-0-9739591-7-8

Tales

of the Heartily Homeschooled

by
Rachel Starr Thomson
and
Carolyn Joy Currey

Table of Contents

Introduction . . . 1

<u>Part One: Make Way for Living</u>

1. Ontario: The Journey Begins . . . 5
    The peace was quickly shattered by a loud bellow. "Are there any more small stuffables? Last call for small stuffables! No? All right, then . . . everybody in!"
2. We Wish You a Currey Christmas . . . 9
    No sooner was the tree decorated then it fell over, flooding the living room with the contents of the tree-bucket and breaking several ornaments. Oh, did I neglect to mention that my father was stuck underneath the tree?
3. Freezing At 85 Degrees . . . 14
    Polar bears, seals, and naked mole rats are suited to their environments. People are not.
4. Hobbits Shall Not Suffer Alone . . . 18
    It is a frightening thing to realize that one's cousins and sisters do not need a wake up call. It makes one think of plots being hatched.
5. Can I Have . . . ? . . . 23
    Babysitting is like playing tennis. The kids stand on one side of the net and fire requests. The babysitter leaps, dives, and swishes to throw the answers right back before something unfortunate happens.
6. The Rutabaga Fest . . . 27
    We Thomsons descended on the world of trade shows like Attila the Hun with a sales pitch.
7. How To Be Funny Without Even Trying . . . 32
    Become an abnormality when it comes to dressing, a sort of hiccup

in the world of fashion, and voila! You're hilarious.

8. Those Bygone Weiner Days . . . 37

> *Merrily and rowdily we hiked along. Suddenly, someone (I suspect it was me) glanced up the mountain and saw a terrible something with a large head, a barrel-like body, and a long nose.*

9. A Mother's Eye View . . . 43

> *Some people have concluded, based on such behaviour, that all mothers are liars. I don't agree with their conclusion.*

10. Pitter-Patter . . . 46

> *Whoever coined the phrase "pitter-patter of little feet" didn't have children. He had mice. Children don't pitter-patter except when they don't want you to know what they're doing.*

11. Bare Foots and Bunting Bags (or, Why Babies Are the Bestest) . . . 50

> *Have you ever stopped to think of the creativity of a God who could invent "cute"?*

Part Two: Family, And Other Oddities

12. Manitoba: The Journey Takes Turns Literary and Life-Threatening . . . 57

> **Morgue, the**, *n.: The van after the massacre of the national bird of Manitoba. Final tally: eleven bumpy human beings with nervous twitches in their eyes; 3,658 dead mosquitoes.*

13. The Battle of Underwear Mountain . . . 64

> *There, tucked away in a corner of Mom's room, the basket languishes for months until Mom announces that it's time to Do Something About It.*

14. Crackers . . . 68

> *People sometimes assume that big families must turn out little cookie-cutter kids, every one exactly alike. The opposite is true.*

15. The December Games . . . 72

> *As exciting as the Olympic games are, they've got nothing on my family of sixty-odd relatives during the holidays.*

16. The Return of the Rings . . . 78

> *Our parents went out one night, and while the younger ones*

> *peacefully reposed in their beds, we settled around the television with great anticipation.*

17. Things That Go Boing in the Night . . . 84
    > *Before I could collect myself and my belongings, the clock struck eleven and the house went "Boing."*

18. Who, Me? . . . 88
    > *"As I was saying: do you think having a big family makes you loopy? Or is it just that some people are more organized than others?"*

19. If It Fits in Your Mouth, Eat It . . . 92
    > *Whatever the reason, Currey children have a propensity to eat weird things, much to our parents' horror and disgust.*

Part Three: War Against the Machine

20. Saskatchewan: The Journey Comes to a Sudden and Tragic End. Almost. . . . 97
    > *We didn't really sit up and take notice until the stench began to remind us of smoke.*

21. Vacuum Cleaners I Have Known . . . 101
    > *I'm a little ashamed to say so, but our vacuum cleaner suffered greatly in its lifetime. Our house is vacuum cleaner purgatory.*

22. Pass the Soda, Pass the Fleas . . . 105
    > *I came home from dance class one day to find that most of our furniture had been moved into my ballet studio.*

23. I Want to Be a Child for Christmas . . . 109
    > *As my mother and all other grown-up people have always known, Christmas is a lot of work.*

24. Mom, the Barbecue's On Fire . . . 112
    > *Becky and I looked at each other. "I think the barbecue's on fire," quoth she.*

25. On a Soggy Sunday Morning . . . 117
    > *The upstairs toilet, caught up in the rush of excitement, also did its part. It faithfully dripped for hours, all through the night.*

26. Put Out the Earthquake, and Go Back To Bed . . . 121
> *In the meantime, my parents were riding their bed across the floor, watching their bunny slippers hop across the carpet in front of them.*

27. To Build a Fire . . . 124
> *All of this was harrowing, but not nearly as bad as the dark and stormy night in Port Coquitlam when our refrigerator held us all hostage.*

28. Apocalyptic Wars of the Computer Age . . . 127
> *Currently we have a PC (Perpetual Catastrophe), which sits in our basement groaning like a card-carrying member of the computer tubercular asylum.*

29. There's Gonna Be a Floody, Floody . . . 131
> *A few frenetic minutes of battle availed us nothing. I bolted upstairs, leaving perfect footprints on the wood.*

Part Four: According to Plan (B)

30. Alberta: In Which We Get Lost in the Scenery and Peer Past Construction . . . 139
> *I had never seen the Rockies before our trip west. As they appeared on the far horizon of the plains, I sat up straighter in my seat and fidgeted with excitement.*

31. Hup! Hup! Hup! . . . 146
> *I'm going to build character whether I like it or not, or else I'm going to fold up and become a dried, useless lump.*

32. Taxi! . . . 152
> *I tried calling the taxi again and—oh, blessed sound—I picked out the faintest hint of a voice amidst the static.*

33. Papa Was a Gypsy, Mama Was a Rock . . . 156
> *It happens every year. The scent of faraway lands rides in with the chilly April breeze, and we are stricken with travel fever.*

34. Charge of the Apple Brigade . . . 172
> *Armed with peeling and chopping knives, cutting boards and garbage pails, we prepared to make a mass charge on the harvest.*

35. Clutter Wars . . . 175
>   *Instead of shrinking, our pile of clutter continues to grow like a man-eating weed.*

36. Faith, Trust, and Windshield Wiper Fluid . . . 180
>   *There is something demeaning to teenage pride about seeing your mother's fingernail marks in the dashboard to the right of you.*

37. Let It Rain . . . 185
>   *There is a scientifically provable link between Thomson family moves and rain. We move, it rains.*

38. Canning Peaches the (Nearly) Painless Way . . . 189
>   *You may not notice that you are in danger of dying from gas fumes because you're flying around like a mad woman cleaning up the disaster. Fortunately, your mother will probably notice and rush in to save your life.*

39. Salvation in the Mailbox . . . 192
>   *I've always looked for salvation in unexpected places.*

40. We're Jesus's People . . . 196
>   *With every lesson comes the growing knowledge that these are the things we believe, the truths that distinguish us. We're different from the world. We're Jesus's people.*

Introduction

This book is our parents' fault.

Had they not believed what the Bible says about children being a blessing and the fruit of the womb being a gift from God, we would not have a tale to tell. The dramatis personae who have made life so very, very interesting up to this point—our combined cadre of eighteen siblings—would not exist. Without them, our lives would be much impoverished.

We, the authors of this book, are second cousins whose families have chosen to walk a fairly counter-cultural road: in numbers of children, in homeschooling, and in various other ways. Through most of our growing up years we lived on opposite sides of Canada with little idea of one another's existence. Then, one fateful day, a relative suggested that we might have something in common.

One of us took the bait. We started emailing. Polite, stunted emails crossed the ether. That is, until the day we discovered each other's sense of humor. The stories began to spill forth: every uproarious family tale we could think of. Eventually, we realized that we could write a book.

So we did. You're holding it now. We hope that you will laugh as you read it. We hope that it will help you look at all the chaotic, beautiful things in your life and see God smiling through them. But we also hope that you will learn to see family in a new way. In writing this, we've opened our eyes anew to all the marvels God has placed in our lives: to the joy of living life in a way that makes room for children and catastrophes, for shared and simple things, and greets it all with gusto.

To our parents, whose steps of faith started all this years ago, we say thank you. To God, whose conductor's hand guides this delightfully messy orchestra, we give glory. The music is beautiful.

Enjoy.

Rachel and Carolyn

Part One:

Make Way for Living

Ontario

The Journey Begins

Rachel:

 Carolyn Currey and I had emailed for two years without ever having met. She lived in British Columbia, I lived in Michigan. We grew close in heart despite the distance, so when the Curreys announced that they were moving to Waterloo, Ontario (a scant four hours north of my house), we were overjoyed. And when it became clear that first, getting together was harder than it sounded, and second, their move would be short-lived and they'd soon be heading west again, we were determined to meet somehow.

 So it was that I found myself in Waterloo the night before the Curreys were due to set out across Canada, ready to pack myself into the van along with my aunt and uncle, eight cousins, two dogs, a hamster, a guinea pig, and a rabbit. When I arrived in the dusk, the house was a-twitter with activity. We went through whirlwind introductions ("Rachel, meet Carolyn, Janice, Dana, Christa, Sara, Andrew, Naomi, and Elyssa . . . family, meet Rachel") and then plunged back to work, packing and cleaning till the wee hours of the morning.

After a few hours of sleep, we were set to wake up again and receive visitors: old friends of the Curreys who had procrastinated their own visit until moving day. They pulled up in their fifteen-passenger van late in the morning and unloaded another tribe of ten children. The movers were due to arrive in an hour or so.

So there we were: ten Curreys, twelve friends, one Thomson (laughing up her sleeve at the familiar absurdity of the situation), a myriad of pets, and a few other friends and family members who'd come to say good-bye—all of us prepared to meet the movers. The movers, I think, were not quite so prepared to meet us.

Tales of the Heartily Homeschooled

Carolyn:

The movers carefully backed the truck down our long laneway, dodging half a dozen children under the age of ten. The supervisor marched into the house, took stock of the situation, and opened her mouth to issue orders. She'd barely had time to say, "Look lively, boys, there must be a zillion beds here somewhere. There are eighteen kids in this house!" before five of the girls (all dancers, small but surprisingly strong), grabbed two fifty-pound boxes or a bookcase each and charged out again. That was the beginning of the end. The hordes descended upon the work. We emptied the house in record time, and the overseer staggered out at the end with her eyes still popping.

The rest of the afternoon was filled with last minute cleaning, visiting, and packing. Once the disbelieving movers had left, more friends and relatives showed up to say good-bye. A few more showed up for supper, and then quietness descended as the population dwindled to a mere eleven.

My dad, the master packer, filled our van with sleeping bags, tents, animals, suitcases, and (most dreaded of all) small stuffables. Mom and a few of the older girls stood out in the field as the sun set.

"I feel like the words 'End of Chapter Whatever-It-Is' ought to appear in the sky right about there," Mom chuckled.

The peace was quickly shattered by a loud bellow. "Are there any more small stuffables? Last call for small stuffables! No? All right, then . . . everybody in!"

Accordingly, we crammed eleven people into the overstuffed vehicle and set off for parts unknown.

We Wish You a Currey Christmas

Carolyn

Christmas is a time-honoured tradition in our family. Christmas carols are wonderful in December, but another song might express it best: "Tradition!" sings Tevye in *Fiddler on the Roof.* "Tradition!" sings our family as we pull out the homemade decorations and recipes we've used for two decades—and especially as we hunt for the yearly foliage.

The Great Christmas Tree Hunt is an important part of Currey tradition. A particular weekend arrives, and my parents hold council to decide whether they should bring home the Christmas tree or wait another week. Excited little children prevail, and the discussion ends several hours later with the entire family pulling on winter paraphernalia as the sun sets. (It's not that Mom and Dad take hours to decide anything, but there have been a few interruptions.)

We reach the tree farm as the last light fades and whip out flashlights. After an hour or so, in which people get lost, fall in the mud, and name half the Christmas trees on the lot, we select one. The tree is christened—"Sir Bulstrode" or "Oswald Bosley" or some other ostentatious title—and is ceremoniously cut down. We haul it back to the van, realize we have no way of getting it inside the vehicle, and somehow secure it to the top with ropes. By the end of the evening the tree stands securely tied to the living room wall, and ten contented Curreys munch cinnamon buns around it.

One Christmas was an utter disaster in the way of shrubbery. After we found and adopted a massive tree, we decided that we would just prop it up in the corner, rather than tying it back as we usually do. Bad plan. No sooner was the tree decorated then it fell over, flooding the living room with the contents of the tree-bucket (large rocks and inordinate amounts of water) and breaking several ornaments.

Disaster ensued as all ten of us tromped around in the newly created lake, getting in each others' way and trying to salvage the ornaments. Oh, did I neglect to mention that my father was stuck underneath the tree? We eventually tied it back, but by that time it had acquired a habit of toppling. It continued to do so throughout the holidays. We tiptoed around the tree whenever we had to go near it. Putting presents under it was like building a delicate puzzle. Every Christmas after that, we have hoped for a better-behaved tree!

Then there is the matter of baking. About twice a year, the baking fit falls upon me. When that happens, nothing can stand in the way of my wooden spoon. Conveniently, Christmas happens to be one of those times. I stalk into the kitchen with a determined look and proceed to crank out about three dozen sweet breads, twenty-four dozen sweet rolls, hundreds of cookies, and copious amounts of candy and cake. This ensures that we don't run out over Christmas. It also lasts us for months. I call to witness the fact that Christa pranced past me on this lovely May day gurgling, "I found another loaf of cranberry eggnog bread from Christmas! How wooooonderful!"

Then comes the mass present attack. We do not do this like most North American families. My father, ever neat and orderly, passes out one present at a time, and we all politely watch the recipient open it. After sufficient oohing and aahing, we pass out another one.

Once a few presents have been opened, Dad calls a halt to the proceedings so we can clean up the wrapping paper. We carefully sort through the paper to make sure nothing of value gets thrown out. Then the paper is piled into two boxes. Two, because my father always unwraps his presents very carefully so the wrapping paper can be reused. The rest of us are not so thrifty, so our shredded paper goes in the other box. We hear that many families get through the pile in an hour or so, but it takes us all day.

For a lot of people, this is what Christmas is all about. The exterior things—the presents, the getting, and that feeling of not being quite satisfied because you already have too much. But this is just like focusing on the wrapping paper rather than what's inside. We often get stuck with the glitz because we've missed the real thing.

The real thing is carefully wrapped up in swaddling clothes and lying in a manger. The whole point of Christmas is the salvation that came into the world so many years ago. Christmas is such a wonderful time to reflect this in our own families. The handmade gifts and bits of folded, coloured paper carry a dear message of love. They are like a mirror reflecting the greater love. Immanuel: God with us.

Freezing At 85 Degrees

Rachel

One day in June I walked two miles, came home, vacuumed, and did stomach crunches for ten minutes. I opened every window in the house and went to get myself a drink of water. When I came back to the living room, Deborah was standing there in a jogging suit, slamming the windows down. "It's *freezing* in here."

God is a perfect planner. He knew people would be lonely, so He put us in families. He knew we'd need to learn the virtue of compromise, so He set each person's internal thermostat differently.

It's not as though we're programmed according to our environments. If this were true, all people in a given location would be hot or cold at the same time, and there would be no reason to fight over the controls on the air conditioner. This is obviously not the case. Polar bears, seals, and naked mole rats are suited to their environments. People are not.

Nor is the hot/cold factor passed on through the genes. I know this for a fact, because Deborah and I have the same two parents (count them: two) and the same four grandparents and the same blue eyes, but we will never ever be comfortable at the same time.

I sleep with my windows open in January. She sleeps under three quilts in July. Someday when we have our own households I'll need special equipment to visit her: a water squirter, heat-stroke medication, and maybe a dromedary.

I don't blame Deborah. It's not her fault. It's just that her internal thermometer thinks 85 degrees Fahrenheit is freezing, and mine thinks the Yukon looks like a nice place to spend Christmas vacation.

We're not the only ones in the family who have this problem. When Mom and I go for walks together, she dresses in everything except her bedding. Mom is very thin-blooded.

Dad, on the other hand, gets hot and sweaty if he does anything as strenuous as, say, starting the car or talking on his cell phone.

Judging from conversations overheard, read, and participated in, I gather that thermostatic incompatibility is a prerequisite for marriage. I've never heard of a couple who agreed on what temperature the house should be kept at or how many blankets should be piled on their bed. (If you've noticed that one of your parents sleeps in a t-shirt while the other one sleeps in a fur-lined parka, you know what I mean.)

Dad's not even consistent with himself. He dislikes living in Canada because it's too cold. The desert he likes—he stays inside all day and cranks up the air conditioning until his children have icicles hanging off the ends of their noses.

Recently I read an article about clothing with personal heating and cooling systems woven into the cloth. This may be the wave of the future, but I wonder whether we really need it. Our skill at compromising may be undermined if we can control our environments to that extent. "That which does not kill me makes me stronger," or so the wise men say. Like most things in a family of any size, temperature discrepancies are one more opportunity for building character.

Thus I say, long live compromise, long live character, and let's *please* turn down the thermostat.

Hobbits Shall Not Suffer Alone

Carolyn

June 2004 was the Summer of the Rings. The movies based on Tolkien's classic had swept us up in a furor of fandom. I translated psalms into Elvish. Dana and Christa began calling each other "Merry" and "Pippin." Sara learned to do her hair in a "Gimli braid." To my chagrin, I was dubbed "The Elf" and called nothing else for months.

In the summers before I was an elf, I established a dance camp tradition. These camps are advertised as "a fun week of dance, choreographing and worshiping God." Well, this is true—but my nice little advertisement leaves out the gory details.

"All right everybody! The sun's up; roll out and start jogging! Breakfast afterwards." The orders change with the day:

"I don't care if it's 4:30 and you've been dancing since nine! Do it again! Next person to talk after lights-out is on kitchen duty for breakfast tomorrow—alone! You spoke. I heard you! Ten push-ups, and let's see some muscle!"

It's not as harsh as it may sound. Dance campers thrive on my rigorous schedule.

When we moved to Waterloo, we decided to hold a dance camp with several dearly loved Ontario cousins. Little did I know what I was letting myself in for. This was not to be a typical tyrannical dance camp experience.

The cousins arrived Saturday night. We snacked, scurried, and held evening devotions, and I shuttled the whole crew off to their tents for the night with strict orders to be silent. No sooner were they nicely stowed away in sleeping bags than the skies poured forth in abundance. This was no quick downpour, either. This was a massive thunderstorm; a forty-five minute celestial waterfall.

Chaos ensued when a bedraggled cousin appeared at the door to report that all the bedding was soaked, and forsooth, the cousins themselves were in little better condition. The order was given: "Dance campers, evacuate!"

In they came like refugees out of the night, slipping and sliding their way to dry mattresses and the promised (or was that "commanded"?) sleep. A couple of girls tried and failed miserably to maintain order in the tents among those who had not yet made the great wet dash. One cousin helped me with soggy things in the garage while another ran things in from the tents with Dana. (Dana fell flat in the mud in her pajamas—poor brave soul, there's always at least one casualty in these matters.)

By Monday night our yard was as dry as Ararat and the girls were back in tents. At seven the next morning I headed out to wake them up. I was still a few yards away from the tents when I heard foreboding whispers.

Now, it is a frightening thing to realize that one's cousins and sisters do not need a wake-up call. It makes one think of plots being hatched. They had piled into a single tent for a good old cousinly pow-wow. As I strolled apprehensively to the tent window, they leapt out of their sleeping bags, raised their right hands with great solemnity, and recited,

> "I am a nice hobbit,
> Not a mindless eating machine.
> If I am to change this image,
> I must first change myself:
> Elves are friends; not food!"

I detected a serious note of challenge to me and my brass-handled whip.

My suspicions were confirmed when Christa kept up her chattering in class even after an ultimatum order of silence. To curb her conversation, I ordered her to do ten push-ups. She complied readily enough. An instant later three cousins and Dana all dropped to the floor and did push-ups with her as they bellowed, "Hobbits shall not suffer alone!" I thought I had invited cousins to dance camp, not half the Shire! But it got worse.

Lunchtime came, and my campers dashed madly for the table. A nose count revealed one or two missing, so I went to hunt for the strays. Upon returning, melodious sounds greeted me. As I came nearer, I realized my proper dance campers were belting out a tavern song from *The Fellowship of the Ring.*

I stalked in with a glare that would have frozen a buffalo in its tracks. Hobbits, evidently, are made of hardier stuff. They gave me a reprise.

Friday came at last, bringing parents for the recital. The girls had worked hard, and they did a really good job. When all was done, they assembled in the living room and began a chant at top volume: "No more push-ups! No more stretching! No more jogging before breakfast!"

On that note, the War of the Rings—er, dance camp—ended. I suppose you could say it was a draw. Let history record that I never surrendered.

(I may have quailed a little . . . but at least they didn't eat me.)

Can I Have...?

Rachel

Babysitting is like playing tennis. The kids stand on one side of the net and fire requests. The babysitter leaps, dives, and swishes to throw the answers right back before something unfortunate happens.

"Can I have a cookie?" whizzes over the net.

"No!" (Whap!)

"Can I paint the house blue?"

"Absolutely not!" (Whiz!)

"Can I stay up past my bedtime and watch TV?"

"Ha, ha, ha." (Sarcastic whap whap.)

"Can I become our family's first three-year-old coffee addict?"

"No!" (Whing—ten points!)

When we pray together at meals, the prayers sound something like this:

"Dear Jesus, thank You for the food and for today and for making me win the race at Awana. Help us have a good day."

"And *me* not to be wetting."

"And help Anna not to wet her pants."

"And no bad dreams."

"And help Tuey not to have any bad dreams. And help me and Jimmy win at the races when we go to nationals and be good sports no matter what happens. In Jesus' name, amen."

"Amen."

"*Ah*-men."

"*I* said *A*-men."

And then Tirzah will look up at me with her plate heaped full of food—at least enough to feed a ravening wolf or two—and say, "Can we have seconds?"

My mental tennis racket comes up, and I want to fire back a resounding "No!" What usually comes out is, "Can't you just wait until you've finished your *first*? My goodness, I've never seen children eat like you." Etc, etc.

They say there are people (on mountain tops, in Tibet) who are content with what they have in life. Those people are not kids. Kids want things. They are not shy about asking for them. Sometimes, we have the opportunity to give them a joyful yes and be as thrilled as they are about it. Sometimes they need to be told no. And no. And absolutely not, not on your life, are you kidding, and if you ask one more time there will be consequences!

Sometimes I realize that I am just as whining and demanding as the younger kids can be.

"God," I say, "I don't trust You to take care of me. I know I have enough now, but what about tomorrow? Can I have seconds? And why won't You let me stay up later, and have more, and be more, and . . . and . . . and . . ."

To be blunt about it, sometimes I'm covetous. To covet is to have the attitude that God has not given us what we need, that He will not give us what we need, and that we must go after it ourselves.

I don't always get what I want. I don't usually understand why I can't have it. Sometimes I'll keep asking, just to make sure God heard me. But like a child who wants to eat all her Easter candy at one sitting, I need looking after, and God does indeed look after me. Sometimes by saying no.

Thankfully, God doesn't have a tennis racket with which to slam my requests back down to Earth. He's so good to me, He loves to catch my prayers and throw them higher until they rain back down on me in showers of blessing. He commanded me to ask so that I can receive. But I'm just as thankful that sometimes I don't.

The Rutabaga Fest

Rachel

When I talk with people for the first time, certain questions tend to come up. Questions asked by quiet, unsuspecting people. Questions like, "How many kids are there in your family?" "Where do you go to school?" "Has your mother been nominated for sainthood yet?" (Or the unedited version of the same question: "Are your parents *insane*?")

Then, of course, there's "What does your father do for a living?" To this I usually reply, "Whatever he wants."

My father is an entrepreneur and as such defies categorization. He does things that involve giant balloons, rock concerts, real estate, and whales. Many of the things he does involve all the rest of us too—especially that paragon of penny-earning, the trade show.

For a couple of years we Thomsons descended on the world of trade shows like Attila the Hun with a sales pitch. We sold a lot of things: little wooden chairs that cure backaches, fudge, music, African baskets, real estate. We never sold a whale, but then again, life ain't over yet. Every weekend Mom and Dad and a few of the older kids would load up the van to the breaking point and drive off to some far horizon, there to set up one, two, or three booths and hawk our wares for a few days.

One summer the trade show crew went to Rhode Island, some fourteen hours from our house. The show was an utter disaster. I heard the customer was nice enough—and all the vendors got a chance to personally try to sell him something—but overall the show was dead with a capital D and lucrative with a capital Broke.

Still, all was not lost. Mom and Dad may have come home short the contents of their wallets, but they brought back a metric tonne or so of carrots, gifted to us by another vendor. And rutabaga. *Lots* of rutabaga.

Now, we like rutabaga as much as the next family with

half a dozen little kids. Possibly even more. But there are limits to how much of the stuff can be peeled, processed, and eaten before the surplus downstairs starts to fertilize the basement floor and grow more little rutabagas.

One sunny day, I cut a wide swath around the rutabaga boxes (which were beginning to put forth, shall we politely say, an odour) on my way up to the kitchen. Mom was standing over the cutting board with a wild look in her eyes. My mother does not generally get wild looks in her eyes, but any vegetable which is peeled by hacking off three-foot outer walls is bound to inspire violence in the meekest of us.

"Growl," she said (or something like that). "We have got to find a way to use up the rutabaga."

"Agreed," I said. "We still have two boxes full, they are growing fur, and by this time," (to be Biblical about it) "they stinketh."

Deborah walked into the kitchen and said, "Does the Strawberry Festival start today?"

Ding! went the little light bulb which appeared, cartoon-style, above my head.

"I have a brilliant idea," I said. "Let's have a Rutabaga Fest."

My mother and my sibling looked at me strangely.

"No, really!" I argued. "It's a wonderful idea. We can advertise in all the local newspapers. We can charge vendors to set up booths on our lawn."

Deborah's eyes sparkled. "We can have a rutabaga cook-off," she said. "Everyone can bring their own rutabagas and . . ."

"No," Mom said. "Everyone can pay us and use *our* rutabagas. The goal is to get rid of them."

"We can play Bobbing for Rutabaga," I said. "We'll have a campfire and sing rutabaga songs."

"Rutabaga carvings," Deborah said. "Everyone can bring their own rutabaga to carve, and then . . ."

"No!" Mom said. "The goal is to get rid of our rutabaga!" She pointed a knife at the half-skewered thing on the cutting board. A dreamy look came over her face. "We can have a huge rutabaga barbecue. It will bring the whole community together. Maybe we can do it every year."

"And," said Deborah, voice resounding with determination, "we can have a competition to see who can grow the largest rutabaga. They'll all bring their own and . . . and . . ."

At this point the conversation broke down. Our dysfunctional committee torched my wonderful idea. It was thrown aside like . . . well, like so much rotten rutabaga. While we were arguing, the rutabaga finished going bad. That night it was taken outside and tossed into the bush for the benefit of the soil and the local wildlife.

What use they're making of it I don't know, but the other night I'm fairly certain I heard the chipmunks singing rutabaga songs.

How To Be Funny Without Even Trying

Rachel

One night, we "big girls" sat around the kitchen table talking about funniness and how to attain it. Some of us are considered naturally funnier than others, and the others in question were bellyaching about it. Why do some people have such a natural flair for the comedic while others couldn't deliver a punchline if they were wearing boxing gloves?

The subject came up while we were reviewing the episode of *Saturday Night News with Muffy Peachblossom* that we shot recently. (With a video camera, not a gun, though some of us would like to take the latter approach lest anyone actually see what we have done.) The episode included interviews with movie stunt men ("We had to jump off a lot of buildings. It really hurt"), actresses, and people on the street

("Lady, that only happens in the moo-vies"). It also included commercial breaks from Cheerios and Darth Lizard of the Salamander's Guild (kindly do not ask).

Anyway, it didn't seem fair that in the course of the video some of us managed to be so screamingly hilarious while others of us tried so screamingly hard to be hilarious and fell flat on our laughing faces. I've given some thought to this, and I have reached at least one conclusion: if you are not naturally Gracie Allen, you will not be funny if you are trying. The key, then, is to be funny by accident.

Jane Austen's *Emma* is an instructive example. Jane Austen's characters are very, very funny, mostly because they are a lot of meddlers who think they know everything and don't. You could be funny as a meddling know-it-all too, but I don't suggest you try it. You may get a few laughs, but you're more likely to get a frying pan wrapped around your head. Besides, the goal is not so much to be laughed *at* as it is to be laughed *with*.

Not knowing what you're talking about is a surefire way to get laughs. We once had a landlord who told us that straw spontaneously combusts when wet. We still split our sides laughing every time we think of it. But again, since he doesn't think spontaneously combusting straw is funny, this isn't the ideal way to become a humourist—you can't enjoy it properly.

Another good way to be funny is to never know what's going on. This one works for me quite often. A little absent-mindedness works wonders. All you have to do is stumble around the house a few times looking for the glasses which are perched atop your head, and you will quickly gain a reputation as "a real funny one."

This is especially useful if you don't pay attention when you're getting dressed. I remember sitting down one evening in a room full of friends. We all took one look at each other's jean skirts, multi-colored socks, and sneakers and burst out laughing. We were a collective fashion disaster. Become an abnormality when it comes to dressing, a sort of hiccup in the world of fashion, and voila! You're hilarious.

In fact, idiosyncrasies in general have a humourous bent to them. These can be idiosyncrasies of the body, mind, or spirit. My bones often crack when I move. Yesterday I climbed the stairs in search of my mother and she called out, "Here comes ol' knickety-knock knees." See? She thinks I'm funny, and I'm not even trying.

One of my friends throws food around the kitchen whenever she cooks anything. Carolyn launches into Shakespearean English whenever she feels strongly about something, particularly if she's trying to rid herself of male attention. Another friend talks to stuffed animals and occasionally attacks people with them. All of these things are funny—and we don't even have to work at it!

The most important thing is that you learn to laugh at yourself. When my grandmother was in college, she wrote a letter home to her parents every day and faithfully posted it. After a couple weeks of doing this, she began to feel hurt that there was no response. She complained to a friend, who accompanied her the next time she posted a letter. When they returned to the dorm room, the friend said, with her eyes twinkling, "Funny how much the trash cans look like the post boxes, isn't it?"

Sending letters by trash can—Grandma laughed so hard she cried. Therein lies the secret of being truly funny: laugh at yourself. Cultivate a sense of the ridiculous in your own life. Before you know it, the whole world will be laughing with you.

Those Bygone Weiner Days

Carolyn

It all began in the days when my parents took five little girls camping in a four-man tent. Other campers stared in amazement as my dad, my very-pregnant-with-Andrew mom, and five small, disheveled girls crawled out of our teeny-weeny tent in the morning—looking a bit like those circus acts when two dozen clowns pop out of a two-person car.

Camping has been a tradition in our family for as long as I can remember, and the memories associated with it are many.

When Andrew was still fairly little we went to Cultus Lake for a week. The temperature exceeded the bounds of decency, but otherwise the trip went quite well. Figuring we were on a roll, we tried a second camping trip in the same summer. We headed up to the mountains that August—a mistake, as we discovered. As the year waned, so did the mountain temperatures. By the end of the trip we had all abandoned our personal sleeping bags and taken to huddling together in the middle of the tent like a pile of shivering kittens.

We had survived far from civilization in two rickety tents twice in one summer, so we figured we could manage two consecutive weeks the next year. We set out to try.

We arrived at Alice Lake on a Sunday night and set up the same two old tents. The first week was a blast. We added phenomenal numbers of "do-you-remembers" to the family archives. I remember standing on my dad's shoulders trying to rig up a tarp as the neighbouring campers looked on and chuckled.

Once we were comfortably set up, all the girls started a plea to go swimming—just as our parents had settled down in their lawn chairs. Andrew, who was three or four at the time, looked up from lolling about and proclaimed, "I'll take them. I'm a grown up."

The next week, a blight fell upon the picturesque scene. Rain clouds rolled in on Monday, and we all cast anxious glances at the sky. That night the skies let loose. It poured ceaselessly for days. Once again we huddled in the middle of the tents, trying not to lie in puddles.

Everyone but Mom and Elyssa ended up in the larger tent. The small tent had been taking colander lessons. Mom set up a reclining lawn chair in the middle of a puddle and tried to sleep with Elyssa, the aerobic sleeper, perched atop her. During Elyssa's nightly acrobatics, the sleeping bag would inevitably end up dragging on the ground. Throughout the night a small lake would seep its way up the sleeping bag.

Dad dug trenches around the tents to keep out the water, but to no avail. At last we came to a conclusion: this was ridiculous! We were drenched, our bedding was saturated, there were no more dry clothes, and we couldn't even cook. We packed up our wet selves and our even wetter belongings and drove out of the campground. Just as we crossed the camp border, the sun came out. We all moaned loudly in protest, but to no avail.

A few years later, we headed for the Okanagan. The weather was lovely, the lake warm, the area beautiful . . . and crowded. We staked our claim in an open, public area—the only place we could find.

In no time at all we became the talk of the place. The campground hosts brought us other campers' forgotten toys, invited us over to pat their dog, told us all the campground news, and delivered hot, buttered popcorn to our tents. We waited in line at the washrooms and listened with a wry grin as total strangers discussed the size, attributes, and behaviour of our family. There are so many of us that no one realized the subjects of their conversation were the people next in line!

An elderly couple in the camper next to our tents watched our every move. It didn't matter what time of day it was. They sat in their lawn chairs quietly observing or watched us from their camper window as they ate dinner.

One fine afternoon, we decided to climb four hundred steps up to the top of a waterfall. We hiked up and then took a path back to our campsite. Merrily and rowdily we hiked along, cracked jokes, threw pine cones, remarked on the view, and made as much noise as a jovial family of ten can possibly make. Suddenly, someone (I suspect it was me) glanced up the mountain and saw a terrible *something* with a large head, a barrel-like body and a long nose.

Everyone else followed my startled gaze. Horrified, we hushed. Dad and Mom cautioned us to stop talking and walk very quietly past the bear. The ten of us tiptoed as silently as we could around the bend, which is how we escaped being mauled, eaten, and otherwise prevented from camping ever again. My astuteness saved the day.

I wish that was the end of the story, but actually, someone decided to take a second look. And then a very hard third stare. From the new angle it was very apparent that we had just pussyfooted past a very cleverly arranged tree stump. (No one remembers who instigated the panic and you won't tell, will you?)

We've been cautioned about so many things in life. When our family became larger than normal, people reeled with horror. We began to homeschool, and mere acquaintances called, begging us not to go through with it. Then there were the just-you-waits. Just wait until they're done high school. No credits? What university will accept them? How will they ever get a job? Your kids will drive you crazy if you keep them home! Just wait until they're (gasp, choke, faint) *teenagers*. Then you'll be sorry.

The just-you-waits, like that bear, have proved to be hollow. So many people dread these life milestones without realizing that they're pussyfooting around something that doesn't really exist. When you find yourself consumed with worry about tomorrow, recall the saga of the bear that wasn't and the stump that was. Don't waste time with worry. There's too much to do today!

A Mother's Eye View

Rachel

On Mom's forty-seventh birthday, Jimmy gave her a homemade card. It said, "Forty-seven years. How did you ever make it?" (Heartwarming, isn't it?)

One thing I know: Mom didn't make it this far without some special abilities in her arsenal. As she opened piles of homemade presents and cards, most of them hastily slapped together five minutes before the birthday celebration, I knew I was watching one such ability in action. Little toys, slips of paper with drawings on them, bits of material sewn together, an enormous pile of scrap-paper cards—Mom oohed and aahed over all of them. She managed to be genuinely excited over what was, quite frankly, a pile of junk.

Every year on my birthday I am presented with a similar onslaught of gifts, and although I thank the givers for them, I can't conjure up the sparkle in my eyes that Mom always gets. My mother is not the only woman with this talent; this special ability that looks at any crayon scribbling and pronounces it a masterpiece (provided, of course, that it's not on the walls). I've noticed it in most mothers.

Some people have concluded, based on such behaviour, that all mothers are liars. Otherwise, how could they look at a card like Jimmy's and say, "That's so sweet"? I don't agree with their conclusion. Not all mothers lie. Mine doesn't. They just see things differently.

My brother Jon used to spend hours digging in the desert dirt-pile we called a backyard. He'd come inside with rusty nails, thorny sticks, and unidentifiable objects in various stages of mangling. They were treasure to him. Mothers can look at the junk hauled in from the dirt and agree that their children have found treasure. They have the ability to wrestle half a dozen scrap-paper-and-packing-tape packages open and become genuinely excited about the contents. They can smile at a little boy and encourage him to *keep* seeing things differently, because that's the magic of childhood, and who wants their children to grow up too fast?

Not all mothers have an equal share of this ability, and not all have it in equal measures from day to day, or even from hour to hour. I'm convinced that it comes straight from God, because God looks at things like a mother. He looks at a widow's mite and says, "That's treasure. That's riches." God looks more at the giver than He does at the gift. And there, I think, lies the secret.

When I turned eighteen, a friend asked if I felt any different. I said no. She told me that when she'd reached that age, she had expected wisdom to magically fall out of the sky and make her an adult. It didn't happen to her, and it didn't happen to me. Remembering that, I think I had better start working now on obtaining a motherly perspective (which is also a godly one). After all, I want to be ready when I get my first scrap-paper card and read those magical words on it:

"Dear Mom . . . how did you ever make it?"

Pitter-Patter

Rachel

"I think this is an error; at best an error of false sentiment, and one that is therefore most often made by those who, for whatever private reason (such as childlessness), tend to think of children as a special kind of creature, almost a different race, rather than as normal, if immature, members of a particular family, and of the human family at large."

- J.R.R. Tolkien, "On Faerie-Stories"

In his essay, dear old Tolkien was talking about children and fairy tales—but his point can be applied elsewhere: there is loads of false sentiment surrounding children nowadays.

Now, I can be just as sappy and sentimental about children as the next girl, but my sentiments have grown out of a life spent with eleven of them. Thus, my ideas are very different from those of people who have confused children with those chubby little angels artists insist on painting, whose wings probably sprinkle fairy dust and talcum powder when they fly.

For example, whoever coined the phrase "pitter-patter of little feet" didn't have children. He had mice. Children don't pitter-patter except when they don't want you to know what they're doing, or when they're sneaking up on you. When, for instance, they all wake up at some unearthly hour of the morning while I'm babysitting.

I lay in bed, deep in slumber, when a pitter-patter in the hallway alerts me to the fact that the children are congregating. I groan inwardly, because in this case "pitter-patter" means, "We're awake, we're starving, and if you don't get up and feed us breakfast in the next five minutes we will pitter the bedroom door down, storm the bed, and patter all over the mattress until you're either up of your own volition or bounced right out of bed."

I sleep in the basement, so I get to hear all the noises feet make over my head every day. I'm pretty good at interpreting them by now. For instance: "Pitter-patter-pitter-patter-*pitter-patter-pitterpatterpitterpatter*--CRASH" means the kids are running down the hallway in socks, sliding across the kitchen floor, and landing in the pots and pans we keep by the back door.

Recently, "Pitter-patter-BOOM-BOOM-BOOM" meant that our teenage girls had been strewn all over the living room floor playing with makeup. Specifically, they were painting half of each face to look like it had just flown in from Zimbabwe while the other half remained relatively normal. Just then a complete stranger (a male one) drove up and knocked on the front door.

The girls did a vanishing act with sound effects. Imagine a buffalo herd on a plywood floor and you'll get the idea. Thirty seconds later they were all in my room, heaving sighs of relief and fiddling with their hair in my mirror.

Our house isn't often empty, but when it is, every little noise starts to echo hollowly. Silence is golden, but after a while even gold can tarnish. Every time a car goes by I jump up, until finally the van pulls up in the driveway. Everyone piles out and comes in, and then the pitter-patter-boom-crash-squeak-squeal-skip-hop of little feet (and big ones) is the most welcome sound imaginable.

Bare Foots and Bunting Bags
(or Why Babies Are the Bestest)

Rachel

"Tabithah." The voice was soft, high-pitched, and slightly lispy.

I cracked an eye open. Sure enough: my baby sister was standing beside my bed, peering into my face from half an inch away. My clock was at a bad angle, so I couldn't see the time, but there was no question that it was earlier than I would have been up on my own.

I grunted.

"Tabithah *cute*," she insisted.

"Mmm-hmm. Hi, Taba."

She leaned over, resting chubby little arms on my bed and smiling confidentially. "Meth."

I sat up. "Mess" indeed. My books and papers were all over the floor. My bookshelf's greatest nemesis had struck again.

She reached up to me. "Up?"

I picked her up and put her on the bed. She grinned and bounced. "Jump, jump, jump. Whee!"

We've always had babies. The name varies, but there's always someone to wake you up in the morning, strew your belongings about, and declare his or her own inherent cuteness. There are twelve of us now, and my parents aren't getting any younger, so Tabithah might be the last. It's a sad thought. Babies are the bestest. I'm not sure what I'll do without them until I can have some of my own.

They say babies are the future. I find it comforting that the future of the world is in the hands of someone who once believed piggy toes were the most interesting things on the planet, and that nothing was more urgent than a snack and a cuddle.

Babies are comfortable being themselves. They don't feel guilty because the world is going down the toilet and they're not doing anything about it. They know it's not time for that yet. Their trust is natural and unthought of, but nevertheless they trust God to choose what is best for them. They're not in any rush to change things.

I love babies because they turn sane adults into googling idiots. People who normally sound like walking dictionaries revert to a sort of hilarious pidgin when they talk to babies. They screw up their faces, smile and coo, and say things like, "There's my wittle punky-wunkin. Hi, bubby-poo! Can you smi-o? Can you? Yay! Gimme a kiss!" And then they present their noses to be slobbered all over. Babies may be one form of pride control, instated by a God who knows that one cannot be entirely puffed up before one's peers when one has recently loved and been loved by someone so humble.

I love babies because they look so cute in bunting bags—and hats, and mittens, and shoes, and dresses, and hair ribbons, and . . . well, they just look cute. All the time. Even when they're crying, they're cute. I often hear people marvel at the creativity of a God who could invent majesty and beauty; music and bird calls; photosynthesis and the segments of an orange. But have you ever stopped to think of the creativity of a God who could invent "cute"? There is something to be learned here about God's sense of value and also about His sense of humour, because cuteness is intrinsically light-hearted.

Babies, I have heard, are God's way of being an optimist. They are His way of reminding us that things are not so bad. Evil may be rampant in this world, but as long as piggy toes are fascinating, bunting bags are adorable, and grown men will bend over backwards to earn a slobbery smile, there is hope for us.

Part Two:

Family, And Other Oddities

Manitoba

The Journey Takes Literary, Life-Threatening Turns

Rachel:

We spent three nights in Ontario before crossing our first provincial border. Into Manitoba we charged, headed for Winnipeg and the Canadian plains. At this point in the trip everyone had settled in for the long haul. Entertainment came in all forms: Carolyn braided my hair and hers, Christa fiddled, Dana wrote new words to the tune of "The Pirates Who Don't Do Anything." I kept myself happy by compiling a mental dictionary of terms special to the trip.

bipolar, adj.: A good description of my feet, one of which was resting on a crock pot (plugged into a cigarette lighter, a crock pot is a delightful but potentially dangerous alternative to cold food three times a day), and the other of which was resting on an ice pack.

bustle, n.: The back end of the fifteen-passenger van, i.e., "The other drivers need to give me room to turn around; this van has quite a large bustle."

Elf, the, n.: Carolyn. This was actually first applied to her at cousins camp, but to her chagrin it remained her usual title throughout the trip. It is used as follows:

> Sara: "Elf, can you pass the gum?"
> Carolyn: "I have a name."
> Sara: "Oh, sorry. *The* Elf."

Iggy the Piggy, n.: The van. It is white, suggesting to the vivid imagination a slight resemblance to an igloo—hence "Iggy." It devours more gas than a 747, hence "Piggy."

mosquito, n.: The national bird of Manitoba.

massacre, n.: What happened when we were attacked by the national bird of Manitoba.

Morgue, the, n.: The van after the massacre of the national bird of Manitoba. Final tally: eleven bumpy human beings with nervous twitches in their eyes; approx. 3,658 dead mosquitoes.

pedestrian extremities, pl.n.: Feet, as in, "Sara, kindly remove your pedestrian extremities from my place of repose." This term is specific to Carolyn.

Pollyanna, n.: Aunt Cathie, who never believed we were lost.

Puddleglum, n.: Uncle Dave, who never believed we were found.

panic, n.: What happens when Pollyanna is driving and Puddleglum is navigating, i.e., "Turn left *now!!!* No, *there!!!* We're lost *again!!!*"

"This Little Piggy," n.: Uncle Dave's favorite game when he wasn't driving, usually involving Carolyn's toes and a lot of shrieking.

van, n.: Supposedly a mechanical contrivance on four wheels, designed for the conveying of people, animals, luggage, and a Christmas tree stand across the Canadian wilderness. In actual fact, a slaughterhouse and the scene of the grisly, grisly deaths of thousands of mosquitoes.

Ygl, n.: Another name for Uncle Dave. This is pronounced "Iggle"; however, it should never be confused with "Iggy the Piggy." Ygl is short for "Your Gracious Lordship." The title is courtesy of Carolyn and gleefully used by Aunt Cathie.

If moving day in Ontario reminded me to make room for people in the messy joy of life, crossing Manitoba reminded me that a sense of humour can get you through anything. Proverbs 15:15 says, "All the days of the afflicted are evil, but he that is of a merry heart hath a continual feast." Cultivate a merry heart, and you can withstand anything: getting lost, attempts to navigate, some people's singing. Even the Attack of the Killer Mosquitoes.

Carolyn:

We entered Manitoba about mid-morning and stopped at a park for lunch under the trees. It was lovely, until some of the local fauna dropped in: mosquitoes, Canadian prairie style. There was serious danger of being consumed for lunch while we consumed our lunch, but somehow we managed.

At supper time we pulled into a lovely rest stop, complete with washrooms, picnic tables, and space for restless legs to run. Best of all, there was no one else there. (No one *human*, anyway. Begin ominous music.) We piled out and unloaded all the supper paraphernalia: dishes, tablecloths, and the crock pot.

In minutes, we knew why this rest stop had been abandoned. Mosquitoes descended upon our van, our food, and our persons as we looked on in horror. The lid of the crock pot was black with them. A mad panic seized us. All the kids dashed for the van. My parents, Rachel, and I scooped up the remains of our dinner and ran for cover. Dad bellowed directions over the collective shrieking. "Don't drop the cutlery! Hey, you left a fork! No pushing! All right, all right, calm down!" You have never seen eleven people and an uneaten supper disappear so quickly.

The van pulled smoothly away from the deceptively lovely picnic area, but inside all was still chaos. We had one goal: exterminate the pestilence! We lunged, squirmed, shouted, gesticulated. Fists flew, pounding mosquitoes against the ceiling, seats, windows, and nearest siblings. At long last a nervous calm descended, broken only by the occasional holler: "*There's one! Someone GET it!*" Oh, the trauma.

Eventually we reached Winnipeg, but we remained generally despondent until morning. Dread of our next destination hung over us: Saskatchewan, reputed to be the worst mosquito province in the nation. Worse still was the threat of low spirits, the natural children of dread. Two hundred kilometers of complaints from eleven mouths might not have had a repellent effect on the mosquitoes, but would likely have made us perfectly odious to each other.

We moped and worried aloud, but then something remarkable happened: the whole situation began to look . . . funny. We giggled as we looked around our blood-spattered van. We joked about morgues, bloodbaths, and mosquito massacres.

By the time we reached Saskatchewan, we had regained our genial mood. We ended up pleasantly surprised by the Saskatchewan mosquitoes, which were few and far between. A merry heart does indeed make a continual feast: though we were itchy and bumpy, we proved it true. And of course, the best thing about a feast is that there's plenty to go around!

The Battle of Underwear Mountain

Rachel

Recently Mom and the big girls donned our bravest spirits and faced down the Dread Laundry Basket.

This is not just any laundry basket. It is the container which holds all unclaimed socks, underwear, and pantyhose in the house. Even in a small family, such articles add up. Imagine the mess in a family with ten girls and two boys, all of whom are very adept at not claiming their personal belongings. Into the basket go items so large that no one is shameless enough to claim them, atrocious apparel in shocking colors, and scads of socks without mates. There, tucked away in a corner of Mom's room, the basket languishes for months until Mom announces that it's time to Do Something About It.

Our Michigan cousins call this a Sock Party. I call it The Battle of Underwear Mountain. Let me assure you, it is not a pretty sight.

The first phase of our most recent battle was particularly ugly. Leah sat cross-legged in the living room and dumped the contents of the basket onto the floor in front of her. Into the melee rushed my sisters; grabbing, pushing, pairing, denying; until Mom called a halt and ordered us to go about the scuffle in an organized fashion. Good thing for Leah. By this time she was buried under everyone's discards, under threat of pulverization if she didn't move.

Next, we moved in to Divide and Conquer. Underwear and tights are easy enough to subdue. Simply force them into neat stacks. Socks are another story. They did their best to confuse us by looking alike but not quite matching, changing length when we weren't looking, and other nefarious schemes. But we got the best of them at last. We paired pairs and discarded discards until the whole lot of them were under control.

Phase Three is especially painful. We all got down on our hands and knees to identify those poor survivors that belonged to us. This is not as easy as it sounds, especially for me. I know that my feet are large, but for some reason I cannot fix the size of my socks in my mind. I really don't know what any of my socks look like, except for the ugly red stretched ones. Even I can identify those.

My problem does not end with socks, actually. When Tirzah was three, she would sit with me while I folded laundry and tell me who everything belonged to so that I could get it all into the correct piles. It's a little embarrassing to have a three-year-old sister with greater powers of observation than I myself possess, but being an eccentric (I'm a *writer*, for heaven's sake), I just don't notice trivialities like clothing.

During this phase we suddenly discovered that someone (Leah again) had neglected to throw away pantyhose that were full of runs, so she and Mom had the task of shoving their hands through them to find out which pairs were wearable and which were not. It was my job to throw the unusable tights out. A large number of them, I believe, once belonged to me.

In fact, I distinctly recognized a number of casualties from The Day My Pantyhose Rebelled—another bone-chilling standoff, which saw fit to take place just before a funeral where I had to dress nicely and stand around in my Sunday shoes all day.

At long last the skirmish ended. We won (we don't always). At this point, we brave soldiers fell into some good-natured squabbling, taking out our last bits of aggression by whacking each other in the arm and protesting loudly.

The conquering of Underwear Mountain, like many another victory in our lives, was achieved through teamwork, discipline, and something resembling organization. I'm sure there's a lesson to be learned here, but I'll leave it to you to find it. I'm off to relax in my newly matching socks, pleased to know that it will be months before we have to do this again!

Crackers

Rachel

Keturah looked askance at Tirzah as she dreamed up an unusual recipe.

"You take hot water and a bowl," Tirzah said. "Then chocolate, so it melts. Yum."

Keturah nodded slowly, struggling to catch on.

"Then you put marshmallows in," Tirzah continued. "And gummie bears . . ."

"And crackers," Keturah said, nodding sagely.

Tirzah stopped short. "No! Not *crackers*!"

People sometimes assume that big families must turn out little cookie-cutter kids, every one exactly alike. The opposite is true. One of the blessings of a big family is that we get to examine the creativity of God up close—because no two of us are exactly alike in any respect, despite the fact that we share parents, upbringing, and circumstances.

This becomes obvious whenever we have to do anything together. Walk, for instance. Becky and I do not walk well together, because she charges down the road like a woman of purpose, while I like to lollygag. She makes tracks, and I stop to look at them.

Shopping is a similar experience. Becky can be in and out of a store in 15.3 seconds. I usually follow along behind, holding groceries which she thrusts at me, tripping on things and humming with the background music. Of course, our divergent personalities do come together in lovely ways. If the background music is good enough, we just might drop the groceries and waltz.

Our personalities often clashed in our trade show days, when we had to set up booths together. The fudge booth for example. Deborah would have it up in three hours: every piece of chocolate in perfect position, every bit of wrapping crisp and professional, every price tag a work of art. Becky would put it up in five minutes and begin hawking fudge before the dust settled. I'd spend forty-five minutes pulling supplies out of boxes and saying, "Wait, what's this again?"

Each member of the family has unique strengths, weaknesses, and quirks. We really don't need a TV for entertainment—it's just as much fun to sit on the couch and watch the family interact. Deborah and Leah line dance in the living room while Becky and I sing old English folk songs in the kitchen; Jon plays battle scenes from *Lord of the Rings* while humming his own soundtrack; and Tirzah jumps around in circles just for the sheer exhilaration it. Micaiah and Keturah dance. Naomi draws and Jimmy hammers at projects in the basement while Anna cuddles with anyone available and Tabithah sits and looks bewildered by it all.

Thanks to my parents, nine sisters, and two brothers, I've learned that individuality is best developed when it is forced to rub shoulders with others. I've learned that we can meet through our differences as well as through our commonalities, as we discover that crackers may be just what the recipe needs.

Together, we are something much stronger—and definitely more interesting!—than we could ever be alone.

The Great December Games

Rachel

During the 2002 Winter Olympics, my family sat glued to the front of our sixteen-inch television screen every night. We watched with bated breath to see which Olympic daredevils would beat their competitors, avoid bashing their brains out, and take home a metal necklace in one of three fashionable colours.

The America-Canada hockey game drew particular interest. My grandparents and uncle showed up with a box of doughnuts from Tim Horton's and parked themselves in front of the TV with hardly a howdy-do. We all had equal claims to American and Canadian citizenship, except for Grandma, who was entirely American, and Grandpa, who couldn't be more Canadian. We all cheered for Canada except Grandpa, who waved a little American flag and nearly got a box of doughnuts pitched at his head.

(In case any of you have short memories or, gasp, didn't *care* about the game: Canada won.)

As exciting as the Olympic games are, they've got nothing on my family of sixty-odd relatives during the holidays. What can be more harrowing than a game of Pack-the-Kids-Into-the-Car-for-the-Hundredth-Time, a breathtaking run of Don't-Spill-the-Jello, the incredible course of Do-All-the-Shopping-On-Christmas-Eve, or a little event I like to call Race-the-Toddler-to-the-Bathroom?

The last of these involves one partially potty-trained toddler dressed in thirty-six layers of winter clothing, one teenage sister, and one mad dash through the darkened hallways of the church where we hold our annual family Christmas party.

It's a triathlon. The first part begins when the toddler looks up with a pained expression and says, "I hafta go potty." The teenage sister snatches up the child and holds it as one would an overstuffed football, then hurtles through a maze of hallways, dodging small children and occasionally knocking heads with another pair barreling in the other direction.

The second part commences when the teenage sister ploughs through the bathroom door and sets the toddler down. While the child does the I-hafta-go-potty dance, the older sibling frantically whips enough clothing off the younger one to clothe a Third World country.

Finally, the toddler is actually placed on the potty. Getting said toddler to go is not always as easy as it sounds. Typically the child balks at being placed on something so imposing as a public toilet. The doing usually does get done, if only out of fear of the red-faced teenage sister with smoke coming out of her ears.

The Thomson family Christmas party is always held in a church, because we outgrew your average house a long time ago. Dad is the oldest of eight siblings. At last count there are fifty-three grandchildren, more than half of them under the age of sixteen.

The day is always filled with feasting, fellowship, foolery, and of course, games. The crowning event of the day is

Try-To-Go-Home. This is a game each of the eight families plays equally well. There are always two teams involved, though how they are divided varies from year to year. Often the division is husband versus wife and children; sometimes wife versus husband; sometimes children versus parents. It's always very exciting. Here's a play-by-play for the benefit of those who have never witnessed the game.

> Husband: "Let's go!"
>
> Wife: "Where's my purse?"
>
> [Husband searches for purse and finds it under two sixteen-year-olds while wife gabs with sister-in-law.]
>
> Husband: "Honey, we have three hours to drive tonight. Let's get going already!"
>
> Wife: "Aren't you forgetting something? Where are the kids?"
>
> Husband: "Freezing in the van waiting for you."
>
> Wife: "No, they're not. See, there's our daughter."
>
> [Husband takes off after daughter and drags her back with half a dozen cousins clinging to her legs. Husband

searches room for wife and sees her pouring a hot cup of coffee.]

Husband: "Honey . . ."

Wife: "Oh look, there's Davey! I haven't even *seen* Davey yet!"

[Wife charges across room to corner nephew. Husband looks at watch and notices another of his children slipping around the corner. He tracks child down and brings her back, then takes wife's arm firmly.]

Husband: "Time to go."

[Wife breaks loose and begins to dance and sing the Good Night Song from *Sound of Music.*]

Wife: "So long, farewell, auf wiedersehn, goodbye . . ."

[Two dozen nieces and nephews and one uncle form a chorus line and start doing the can-can. Husband shakes head and reaches down to catch son, who is darting underneath his legs. He picks struggling child up and casts a weary glance at the chorus line, which is now singing "Old McDonald" with great vigour and vim. Husband sighs and turns to engage brother-in-law in theological discussion.]

Ten minutes later . . .

[Wife passes by wearing coat and gloves with three children in tow. Shakes head.]

Wife: "Honestly, will he never learn? Now we'll never get out of here."

The only thing missing from The Great December Games is an awards ceremony. One of these days maybe we'll institute one. Until then, we'll continue to play with all our might and look forward to coming back next year, provided, of course, that anyone succeeds at leaving in the first place.

The Return of the Rings

Carolyn

The year 2004 was a momentous one for the house of Currey. First, because we made our third cross-country move. Second, because the movie *Return of the King* was released to theatres. Some of my sisters would say I should reverse these two events to place them in order of importance.

As the release date approached, excitement in our house rose to a fever pitch. Finally, the long-awaited day arrived. Our grandparents took us to the theatre. The movie was all we had hoped, in most cases matching the book quite well. It was dramatic, fantastic, and terribly sad. The bittersweet ending depressed Dana and Christa for weeks. We spent the drive home restoring Christa to equilibrium. She had pulled her hat down over her face in deep mourning.

The scene:

Christa: "I can't believe they ended it that way! It's over! And poor Pippin was crying! And Frodo is gone! And . . . oh!"

Carolyn: "Wonderful. Now we have a depressed Took on our hands."

Dana: "Would you like a potato chip?"

Christa: "*No!* I *hate* potato chips!" (Moans and groans from under the hat.)

Dana: "What about raisins?" (Christa's favourite.)

Christa: "*Yuck!* Raisins are horrible! I never want to see another raisin again!"

Carolyn: "This sounds serious. Christa. Breathe deep and calm down. It's just a movie."

Christa and Dana, in chorus: "It's not *just* a movie!"

Dana: "It's the greatest movie of all time! Christa, do you want salsa?" (Another Christa favourite.)

Christa: "I *hate* salsa!" (Sniff, sob, snuffle.)

Dana: "Well . . . what about . . . a chip!"

Christa: *"I hate chips!"*

At this point Christa launched her head forward blindly into space. Her hat was still over her face, which prevented her from seeing the chips Dana was holding in front of her nose. The chips exploded all over the car. Janice, Dana, and Christa exploded with laughter in the back seat. Yes, even Christa, in spite of herself. Our grandfather's eyebrows signified his disapproval of the mess, so I confiscated her hat until she cleaned up every crumb.

Shortly after that traumatic experience, Mom and Dad made the final decision to pack up and move back to BC. Our usual custom when making cross-country moves is to sell all the furniture to pay for the gas. We decided to hold a massive yard sale and bring in as many customers as possible. Before the big day, Dad adorned the telephone posts with yard sale signs for blocks around. Mom placed an advertisement in the Pennysaver.

Around the same time, *The Return of the King* came out on DVD. Christa shrieked with delight when her cousins presented it to her as a birthday present. Our parents went out one night, and while the younger ones peacefully reposed in their beds, we five oldest settled around the television with great anticipation. Sara was especially excited as she had not accompanied us on that memorable excursion to the theatre.

We all watched, breathless, as the inevitable and terrible climax approached. About halfway through the movie, all the characters were in desperate straits. Things could only go up from there, but oh, the suspense!

Suddenly, the phone rang. I paused the movie and dashed to the phone to get the interruption over with. A strange, heavily accented voice came over the line.

"Hello? I'm calling about the ad in the Pennysaver."

Instantly I snapped into helpful and professional mode.

"Yes?" I asked.

"You have cheekens?" the voice queried.

"Pardon me?" Surely I wasn't hearing right.

"Cheekens!" the voice insisted. "This is yard sale, you have cheekens?"

"No. I'm sorry, no chickens." I was thoroughly bewildered by now. All right, so this is a newcomer to Canada—but do they really sell chickens at Chinese yard sales?

At this point, an unsettling noise came over the phone. To my horror, it was laughter—very familiar laughter. My honoured and revered mother was seriously splitting her sides on the other end of that line. I roared and bellowed, much to the curiosity of my siblings, who still thought I was dealing with a business call.

When I threatened to hang up, she told us to turn off the video and go to bed. Somehow the other girls managed to figure out what she'd said. We all fought for the phone in a mad attempt to give our reasons why we should be permitted to finish the video.

"Sara's never seen it!"

"It's at the worst part!"

"I'll never sleep!"

"We'll get up at 5 a.m. and finish it and that will be even less sleep!"

But to no avail. To heap sauce upon chicken, we were packed off to bed. In this clash of the Rings—Tolkien versus the telephone—we learned one important lesson. Though the fate of Middle-Earth may hang in the balance, the truly important things still prevail: sleep, mother's orders, and of course, cheekens.

Things That Go Boing In the Night

Rachel

I sat on the couch with a cup of tea in my hand, engrossed in *The Strange Case of Dr. Jekyll and Mr. Hyde*. The kids had long been in bed, the house was clean, the only sound was the ticking of the clock on the wall. I turned a page and glanced up.

The clock read 10:59.

A cold chill ran through me. I had stayed up too late. I should have safely cloistered myself in my room twenty minutes ago. I slapped my book down and swung my legs around, scrambled to my feet, and snatched up my tea—but I was too late. Before I could collect myself and my belongings, the clock struck eleven and the house went "Boing."

My sisters sometimes call 11:00 the hour of their "night raids." It is also known as Pandemonium, Hyper Hour, and Utter Madness. It is the hour in which the usually calm and placid older set of Thomson children goes completely nutso. It is the Descent Into Chaos, in which no cup of tea or peace-loving oldest sibling is safe.

The floor shook under me as teenagers hurtled down the staircase. I jumped to one side, spilling precious drops of hot tea on my hand. Deborah collapsed shrieking on the couch I had just vacated, Becky tickling furiously. Deborah's long legs kicked as she fought off the onslaught. I made for the kitchen door just as Leah sprinted in from the basement with a tin of cookies, Naomi bellowing behind her and brandishing a large wooden spoon.

"Come *back* with those! They were a *surprise!*"

I looked to Mom to help me escape, but she was in the easy chair laughing fit to kill. My book had already been rolled over. I said a prayer for its safety as I sidestepped the whoosh of the wooden spoon. My tea jarred and spilled all down the front of my sweater and jeans. I looked scathingly at the culprits, but they were kickboxing, so they didn't notice.

During the day we all work hard, taking care of kids, the business, and the house. At 11:00, my sisters unwind. Take a can of Coca Cola, kick it around like a football for an hour, and then open it. You'll get an idea of what this species of "unwinding" looks like. It is the hour of tickling, line dancing, karate, and Muffy Peachblossom. Muffy Peachblossom is Becky's alter ego, a television talk show host who wears her hair flopping in her face, simpers at the camera, and talks with a pidgin English accent.

I used to wonder if this happened in other homes. Do other normally responsible sets of young people lose their sanity late at night? I escaped downstairs to the computer one night recently, cup of tea safely cradled in my hands, and got online to talk to Carolyn. The conversation trotted along nicely until, suddenly, I heard the echo of a "boing" across the miles.

"Raaachel!" Carolyn's email howled. "Everyone's playing with my ballet bun, and I don't liiike it!"

A moment later another email arrived: "Since I have written to you I have shrieked and kicked and waved my arms about like a madwoman and punched every single one of my sisters (except the two little cute ones). Hoy! Janice bit me."

I am convinced. There are no safe places on earth when it comes to this sort of thing. We could go live on a mountaintop without siblings . . . but frankly, I'd be afraid to take such a drastic step because, well, I might get bored.

Who, Me?

Rachel

"You know, Mom," I said as I tucked the cheddar cheese safely away in the tea towel drawer, "people have some funny ideas about the dynamics of big family life."

Mom looked up from her paperwork, which she was doing on the kitchen table amidst the wreckage of lunch. I had been enlisted to clean up.

"Oh?" she said.

"Well, for example, they think it must drive mothers batty to have to keep track of everything. Like you're not capable of keeping your head together." I chucked a load of dirty silverware into the dishwasher and grabbed a cup from off the counter. I tipped it upside down, and water gushed out all over my feet.

"Oops," I said.

"Having so many kids does create distractions," Mom said, peering through her reading glasses at the open dishwasher. "Are you sure the stuff in there was dirty?"

I looked down at the sparkling glasses with tell-tale hot water puddling on top. "Oh. Um . . . no."

I crouched down and started going through silverware. One knife plastered with peanut butter, one mayonnaised spoon that splattered when the water gushed out and hit it . . .

"It's dirty now," I said.

"Uh-huh," Mom said, looking back down at her paperwork.

"Have you seen my glasses?" I asked as I pulled a plate out of the dishwasher and examined it. One lone crumb. I scratched it. It was stuck. "I've been looking for them all morning."

"You're wearing them," Mom said.

"Am I?" I blinked. "That's odd." I finished scratching the crumb off and stuck the plate in the cupboard. "Speaking of odd, did you do something special to the chili you left for us to eat last night when you went out?"

Mom looked up, sighed, and took off her reading glasses. "I didn't make chili," she said.

"Well, that's what Dad fed us."

"What was it in?"

"A blue Tupperware container."

"That was spaghetti sauce, dear."

"Oh." I blinked again. "It was good. Anyway, as I was saying . . . do you think having a big family makes you loopy? Or is it just that some people are more organized than others? You know what I mean—an organized person will have an organized big family, and a disorganized person won't."

I poured the leftover gravy into a pitcher and stuck it in the fridge. I poked my nose inside. There wasn't much room left for the peanut butter. I started rearranging things.

"Hey!" I said. "I think I found Dad's wallet."

I exchanged the wallet for the peanut butter and gave it to Mom. I pulled a glass out of the dishwasher and reached into the fridge, pouring myself a tall drink.

"So what do you think?" I asked, bringing the cup to my mouth. "Good heavens, what am I drinking?"

"Gravy," Mom said.

"It's better on meat," I said.

"I think you're right," Mom said. "Some people are just more absentminded than others."

"You know," I said, as I threw the compost out the window and brushed bread crumbs into the compost bucket, "someone asked me the other day if I was losing my mind."

Mom smiled. "Are you?"

I sat down. "Only after lunch."

If It Fits In Your Mouth, Eat It

Carolyn

Perhaps it has to do with our creative streak. Maybe it's related to our natural curiosity. Whatever the reason, Currey children have a propensity to eat weird things, much to our parents' horror and disgust.

Christa shovels pepper onto her food (including her ice cream) by the cupfuls. Dana experiments with grape jelly and mustard sandwiches. Andrew is of the opinion that no dish is complete without a good dose of peanut butter. At least all of these examples are food! Some of us have indulged in stranger things. Glass Christmas ornaments. Dog food. Grass. Glue sticks. Erasers. The list goes on.

Dana doesn't just eat strange things, she wears them. One evening, in a fervour of helpfulness, she gave the French dressing bottle a good shake. The lid was not on properly. That

French dressing ended up all over the floor, the walls, the ceiling, and Dana. A couple of months later, she repeated the performance with garlic ranch.

Christa's strange taste in food has sometimes gotten her in trouble. Whenever she heads off to work, she assembles something that resembles a sandwich. Two slices of bread liberally slathered in mayonnaise, pepper, ketchup, salsa, pepper, curry powder, pepper, a thin tiny little piece of cheese, and whatever other condiment she can find in the fridge. Oh, and did I mention pepper? One evening she made a couple of sandwiches like this and left one in the fridge. Somehow it made its way into my Dad's lunch box.

I've dared to hope that this family peculiarity would be restricted to the middle children. My hopes were dashed today as I heard Naomi sweetly request, "Could I have a ketchup and mayonnaise sandwich? With some pepper?"

As I said, not everything we eat is technically edible. Janice probably takes the honours in this department. The local poison control center got to know us quite well in Janice's younger days. Once she ate berries in the backyard that were unfit for human consumption. Before long she topped that escapade by sucking Daddy's ink pad. I'm sure her insides are permanently stained black.

Her greatest feat, however, was when she ate a Christmas ornament off of the tree. I'm not talking about one of those nice little Styrofoam balls covered with thread. This was a genuine glass Christmas ball. In a frenzy, Mom called poison control, described the disaster with all its lurid details, and asked what on earth she should do.

There was a short silence on the other end. Then, "She *ate* a glass Christmas ball? Is she bleeding?"

The answer being in the negative, poison control hemmed and hawed and finally came to the conclusion that she would probably suffer no ill effects if she hadn't already. (Such wisdom!) None of these outlandish things ever harmed her. Talk about an iron constitution!

I suppose she comes by it honestly. It still disturbs me, though, when I see signs that read, "You are what you eat."

More pepper, Christa?

Part Three:

War Against the Machine

Saskatchewan

The Journey Comes to a Sudden and Tragic End.

Almost.

Carolyn:

A strange smell began to pervade the van as we perambulated over the prairies toward Regina. We paid it little mind, except to discuss whether its source was a nearby factory or a passing vehicle. We didn't really sit up and take notice until the stench began to remind us of smoke.

We had left Winnipeg on the fourth day of our journey and settled in for a normal, uneventful day on the road. We stuck some hot dogs in the crock pot, ostensibly for supper. In truth, we were curious. What happens to hot dogs when you crock pot them, anyway? We figured as long as they came out cooked, we could eat them.

Now, as the smell grew worse, it suddenly struck Mom that its source just might be our supper. She flung pillows, blankets, books, maps, and snacks away from the cigarette lighter in a wild attempt to save us from conflagration. Sure enough, the adapter was smoking madly. She yanked it out, rolling down the window with one hand in order to pitch the thing out should it burst into flames.

The van swerved wildly from one side of the highway to the other, evidence that Dad was about ready to go crazy. An emergency was happening two feet away and he couldn't even look to see what was happening! Mom attempted to calm him down, drive mentally for him, prevent a bonfire, and take care of her burnt fingers all at the same time.

It was the most harrowing five minutes we had yet experienced, but we survived. Sadly, things didn't look good for the hot dogs. The adapter was shot, and we had no other way of cooking them.

That night we pulled into a church in Regina. It was a small church in the upper story of a building with few windows. We ate apples and sandwiches for supper, but we still figured there was, "No sense in wasting good hot dogs." We plugged the crock pot into an old-fashioned outlet in the wall and left it overnight. By the next morning the place smelled like a processed meat factory. (It probably still does.)

At lunchtime the next day, we pulled two varieties of meat from the pot. The outer layer of hot dogs was dry, black, and shriveled. They looked like something one might bring on an expedition across the Sahara. The under-layer was saturated in grease; the hot dogs bloated to about twice their normal size. They dripped as they were removed from the pot.

We ate them. We were hungry and curious, and by George, no hot dogs were going to get the best of us. A few brave souls even came back for seconds.

Rachel:

Somewhere in this world I think there's a family whose roof never leaks; whose car never breaks down; whose crock pot never explodes. A simple and happy life they lead. In my own family, the story is quite different. We are perpetually at war with the machine. Every inanimate object that enters our life eventually takes up arms against us.

Besides providing us with hundreds of amusing stories to tell our grandchildren, this at-war dynamic has a few lessons for us. People are important; objects are not. Relationships last; objects slip, shatter, blow up, burn down, and disappear. "Lay not up for yourselves treasures on earth," Jesus said, "where moth and rust doth corrupt, and thieves break in and steal."

None of our stuff is worth getting upset over, as we'd know if we didn't set our hearts on it. We are to lay up treasure in heaven, and in the meantime, keep fighting the barbecue, begging the car to start, flinging flaming adapters out windows, and laughing.

Especially laughing.

Vacuum Cleaners I Have Known

Rachel

I suppose most of us entertain dreams of glory at one time or another. Even those of us who should be content to live quiet, plebeian lives. Thus we ignore the fact that our lives are a vapour in the wind: ashes to ashes, dust to dust. We might get on better if we dropped the dreams of glory and took joy in doing our jobs. I wax on about this now, because I wish I'd told it to our vacuum cleaner before it kicked the bucket with such high dramatics.

When we bought this particular item, we didn't know it was anything special. We figured it was just a usual vacuum cleaner, destined to live out its usual vacuum cleaner days of sucking, pushing, and breaking down until it was laid to rest on a heap of other appliances one day.

We were wrong.

I'm a little ashamed to say so, but our vacuum cleaner suffered greatly in its lifetime. Our house is vacuum cleaner purgatory. We have fourteen people in our family, and ten of them have hair over a foot and a half in length. When we haven't cleaned the carpet in a while, you can pick out hair in tangled clumps.

Besides the hair, we have twenty-eight booted feet to track mud, one hundred and forty fingers to crumble food and drop things, and fourteen absent minds to not notice the mess until it has been pounded thoroughly into the carpet by the aforementioned twenty-eight feet. The vacuum cleaner bravely endured all this. Once in a while it buzzed, let off burning rubber odours, or dropped things back onto the carpet well wrapped in hair—but mostly it was a good sport.

That all changed one day when I was vacuuming the living room floor with great gusto. The machine began to vibrate till I feared my arm would fall off. "I-I-I th-think there's someth-th-thing wrong wi-with the v-v-v-acuum cleaner," I called to my mother. It continued to vibrate until every part of me went numb. (My toes are still regaining feeling.) Then it blew up.

Well, okay, it didn't actually blow up. It sparked and smoked and whirred and buzzed, and I yanked the cord out of the wall seconds before the actual explosion. I suppose this was cruel of me. Here was our vacuum cleaner, determined to go out in a blaze of glory, and I pulled the plug. There's something pathetic about an interrupted martyrdom. I would have been more sensitive to the poor belaboured creature's feelings; it's just that I was standing in close proximity to it. Blazes of glory are all well and good, but I wasn't quite ready for death by vacuum cleaner. For one thing, it would look ridiculous in a coroner's report.

I do know, however, that the vacuum cleaner *would have* blown up if I had left it alone. I know this because my cousins had the same model, and it also began to spark and smoke in tragic desperation one day. They, like me, pulled the plug; and when their father came home from work he plugged it back in again to see what was wrong. It blew up.

That vacuum of ours had spirit, and though I would not allow it to take me with it, I admire its determination to go up in glory. It ended its days in our closet, ignored. One day perhaps we'll plug it back in and let it have its way. Ashes to ashes, dust to dust.

Pass the Soda, Pass the Fleas

Carolyn

I came home from dance class one day to find that most of our furniture had been moved into my ballet studio. I barely had time to raise an eyebrow about this before I was put to work: not on moving furniture, but on exterminating things that might have been living under it.

We had just moved into our new house when we discovered that we had joint ownership: we were sharing our domicile with fleas. My bedroom was downstairs where the previous owners' dog had stayed, and in no time flat I had itchy red bites up to my knees.

We finally decided that Something Had to Be Done. We tried store solutions, but they didn't work at all. We then applied more unconventional methods. We sprinkled the floors and furniture with a liberal dose of Borax, but our fleas must have been especially hardy, because they stayed.

We were getting a little desperate. Finally my parents bought massive amounts of baking soda and salt, mixed them together, and chucked all the furniture into my studio so the mixture could be applied to the carpets without impediment. We all set to work manually grinding all of that baking soda and salt into the floor.

The method is as follows:

Step 1. Sprinkle a liberal amount of the mixture over two square feet of the floor.

Step 2. Walk up and down over those two square feet for about ten minutes, being sure to rub your feet very hard over the floor.

Step 3. Ask if you can move on to the next area.

Step 4. Continue to grind the mixture into the floor until neither baking soda nor salt can be seen. (You can guess the answer to the earlier question.)

Step 5. Continue method with all flea-infested carpets, couches, mattresses, and other upholstery for hours—and hours and hours and hours.

Step 6. Start vacuuming. This will take awhile, as it is necessary to vacuum each area for as long as it took to grind in the mixture in the first place.

Step 7. When it is about 11 p.m. and you feel like moving out, continue with the same method for hours—and hours and hours.

Step 8. At about 2 a.m., make a bed on the couch and crash until early morning, when the little ones, who have had a very restful night, will come in and bounce you awake.

Step 9. Finish vacuuming downstairs. Then powder, grind, and vacuum the stairs and the second floor of the house, just for good measure.

Step 10. Stomp your foot and yell, "I hate baking soda and I hate salt and I hate fleas and I hate vacuums and I hate carpets and I hate upholstery and I'm moving out!"

Step 11. Decide that bellowing doesn't do a thing to extinguish fleas or speed the work, and keep stomping baking soda and salt into the carpets.

Two weeks later, we discovered that our work had been successful. No more fleas! No more baking soda! No more furniture in inconvenient locations!

Years passed. The great flea stompede receded into the archives of laughable memories. Then, a few months ago, Janice's dogs attacked a stray cat. The cat was rescued, cradled, and brought into the house. I now have itchy red bites up to my knees.

I'm thinking about moving out.

I Want To Be a Child For Christmas

Rachel

My shopping list this December is a mile long. Deborah and I are working with the little kids in the Christmas choir—prepare for a millionth rendition of "Away In a Manger," please.

As my mother and all other grown-up people have always known, Christmas is not merely a season of carols and chestnuts roasting on an open fire. Christmas is a lot of work.

Sadly, in the midst of all the work, I seem to be lacking in the "wonder" department. I am usually very enamoured with Christmas. I remember sneaking into our closet sometime in November when I was a little kid, hoping to unearth our beautiful porcelain Nativity set. Holiday spirit would usually strike me right around the year's first frost, and I'd be a bundle of anticipation right up until that fateful moment when we had nothing left but mounds of wrapping paper and a sink full of dirty dishes.

In past years, though, things have changed. It no longer seems to matter whether or not it snows in time for December 25, or if all my cousins can make it to our family get-togethers. The bands of holiday commercialism and stress are tightening around me, whether I like it or not.

But this year, I plan to rebel.

This year, I will skip through parking lots singing "Deck the Halls" at the top of my lungs. I will say "Merry Christmas" to complete strangers and ooh and aah over useless junk in the store windows, just because it sparkles and looks pretty. I will watch *A Charlie Brown Christmas* and all 3,000 versions of *A Christmas Carol*, taking care to enjoy them all. I will dodge mistletoe, eat pie, and wrestle with cousins, brothers, and sisters—and I will not worry about having better things to do.

Welcome back, Christmas spirit.

I will spend hours studying our Nativity set. (I still have a fascination for those things.) I will drink eggnog and pray that it snows, and when I sing "Hark, the Herald Angels Sing," I will listen to the words.

Oh, I know I'm supposed to be grown up and mature. And there may not be anything *too* spiritual about eggnog and Ebenezer Scrooge.

But I really don't think Jesus will mind. He was once a child for Christmas, too.

Mom, the Barbecue's On Fire

Rachel

It was early autumn in the Mojave Desert, where we lived in a mobile home in a pit-stop of a town called Littlerock. Becky and I marched outside armed with a pancake flipper and a roasting pan full of hamburger patties, determined to barbecue or bust.

It was a little windy out, in a blow-your-gate-off-its-hinges sort of way. This was due to a rip-roaring quirk in the weather called the Santa Ana winds. We had moved to California mistakenly believing that the weather was gentle and mild. It may be so on the coast, but the desert is another story. Less than a month before, had we wanted to barbecue hamburgers, no grill would have been necessary. We could have slapped the patties on the driveway and watched 'em fry.

Come fall, however, desert weather reminds one why it's not so bad to live out there—balmy days, incredible star views, and distant mountains make up for a lot.

So Becky and I headed outside, determined to soak up the sunshine and make a dinner worthy of remembrance. Once outside, I plunked myself into a lawn chair and let Beck, the hamburger expert, work her magic.

The wind, however, seemed determined to keep dinner at bay. When at last we managed to light the barbecue, it flared up into a little inferno, tongues of fire licked every which way by the wind.

Okay, so this had happened before. We could handle it. Becky shut the barbecue lid. We watched incredulously as the fire escaped out the air holes and danced its merry way over to the wooden shelf on the left side of the barbecue.

Becky and I looked at each other.

"I think the barbecue's on fire," quoth she.

"Looks like it," I said, nodding.

"We should do something about it," she added.

"Mmm-hmmm," was my helpful answer.

At this juncture the fire was really getting a little out of control, so I turned and went inside, where Mom was relaxing in a chair.

"Do we have any buckets? I need some water," I said.

"What for?" she asked, looking up with one of those frowns that can be translated as meaning, "Now what have you done?"

"The barbecue's on fire," I said. "Sort of."

"What do you mean it's *sort of* on fire?" Mom asked, her voice raising. "Is it on fire or isn't it?"

"Well, we can't really tell . . . but the fire's quite high. I'm pretty sure the hamburgers are going to burn." At this point someone produced a bucket, so I filled it with water and hurried back outside.

When I got back, Becky was sitting on the ground next to the barbecue, while the fire raged above her.

I threw the water over the inferno and, failing to put it out, asked, "What are you doing?"

"I'm turning off the gas tank," was her tight-lipped explanation.

At this point the flames licked down and caught the gas hose on fire, and our eyebrows shot up, hit the clouds, and bounced back down to our faces, where they nestled like alarmed caterpillars. Becky's fingers began working all the harder at their chosen task, and I raced back inside.

"More water?" someone asked.

"Yes, the barbecue is definitely on fire," I said. "Actually, I think the gas hose just caught . . ."

The rest of the incident is smudged in my memory like a bad inkblot on stationery. I believe that my parents threw a conniption and Dad raced outside to save the day. The hamburgers, as my stomach still laments, did not survive. Nor did the barbecue. But we learned a valuable lesson:

Do not, on a windy day—outside, in the desert—light a fire.

Homeschoolers learn this sort of lesson a lot, because they live by a dangerous credo which states that people learn best by doing. Cook a hamburger for yourself, and you'll never forget how. Blow up the house, and you're not likely to do it a second time. You see? Lessons. In a homeschooling family, every disaster has a unit study.

Our fire lessons aren't always so life threatening. Lately Dad's been teaching the boys to build a fire in our very, very old fireplace, which smokes rather more than it should but makes everything cozy and warm in this household of ours. They get fuel wherever they can find it: leftover newspapers from their delivery routes, cast-off branches from the trees in the backyard, and, uniquely, holiday leavings. Dad's favourite fuel coincides with our need to put the house back in order after December, and I think we should tune the smoke alarm to play the new family anthem: "Hail the Christmas Tree, Merrily Burning."

I'm very grateful for all the lessons I've learned in life, and not only the "life-and-death" variety. Most of them, after all, have been of the pure "life" variety. Just as people learn best by doing, they also *live* best by doing—by laying aside worry, canning procrastination, and plunging right in for the long haul. Disasters and ominous barbecues aside, there's a life full of lessons ahead of us all. I, for one, am glad to be living it.

On a Soggy Sunday Morning

Carolyn

Sunday morning in our house is a mad dash to get dressed, do eight heads of long hair, deal with dogs, rush through last minute tidy-up (nothing is ever done when it looks like it's done—there is *always* last minute tidy-up), and get out to church on time. Everyone must do their part. Especially if, as on the day in January when this story takes place, we are expecting forty people to come over after church and help us celebrate Naomi and Elyssa's joint birthday party.

We had just moved into the little town of Agassiz, British Columbia, so we didn't know our guests very well. Understandably, we took more care than usual with preparations. Food and house were readied the night before. We felt so organized. Everyone, I reiterate, did his or her part.

Teams were organized for cleaning, baking, and games preparation. No one was exempt.

The upstairs toilet, caught up in the rush of excitement, also did its part. It developed a large crack and faithfully dripped for hours, all through the night. When this house was designed, it was fashionable to have carpet in the bathrooms. Completely impractical. When we awoke, the floor was soaked in a very large, spongy circle around the toilet.

I cleverly avoided the mess by dressing in the downstairs bathroom, where I found that the water from above had soaked through the floor—enough of it to drip down the back of my neck and alert me to the problem. The ceiling got my full opinion of the situation, its behaviour, and its appearance in general. (Have I mentioned that I frequently converse with inanimate objects? Sometimes they deserve a good chiding.)

I exited as hurriedly as possible, glaring at the offending portion of our domicile's structure. It looked back forlornly out of holes where plaster had fallen and wallpaper hung in strips.

On further inspection, we discovered that the water had leaked underneath the downstairs cabinet and into the closet in the adjoining room. As we took all this in, someone mentioned that church started in less than three hours.

We set to work in our pajamas: mopping floors, cleaning carpets, and putting out buckets for further spillage. Early Sunday morning found my poor Dad kneeling in a puddle fixing the toilet while the rest of us mopped, yelling at each other to get more rags and buckets. The result was that seven of us yelled while the three littlest kids wandered around, hopelessly trying to find cleaning supplies!

At the end of this tremendous effort, we had tidied everything up and temporarily patched the toilet. Not much could be done about the wallpaper and ceiling in the downstairs bathroom, so we just hoped no guests would go in there.

Our house was in reasonable condition when people arrived, and the party was a success. The plan was to keep the events of the morning undercover, but certain people in our family have quite the sense of humour. By the time the party was over, everybody knew about and had laughed over that morning's chaos.

Moral of the story? Never feel too organized at nightfall, for thou knowest not what thy bathroom doth plan for the morning!

Put Out the Earthquake, And Go Back to Bed

Rachel

We moved from Ontario, Canada, to California the year that I turned thirteen. We spent a few weeks living in a hotel room and then moved into a big house in a ritzy neighbourhood in the San Fernando Valley.

The community where we rented a house was called Northridge, as we smilingly informed those who wanted to know. But a shadow quickly fell across our joy. Every time we told someone where we lived, they grew pale. Their eyes shifted nervously.

"Isn't that where the *big* earthquake was a few years ago?" they would ask.

Through such unnerving conversations, we discovered that a large earthquake had struck Northridge just four short years before. In fact, the area was still suffering aftershocks. We took this information in with slight bewilderment. As we were easterners, earthquakes were entirely foreign to us. Our natural disaster instincts all involved running down into the basement, and in an earthquake, that is a manifestly bad idea.

I woke one night to the sound of the blinds rattling sharply against my window. In fact, the window itself was rattling—as were the bed and the bathroom mirror. I've sometimes thought it would take an Act of God to get me out of bed when I'm really tired, but evidently it takes more than that. I just opened my eyes, thought to myself that we were having an earthquake, and decided that sleep would be the most pleasant way to wait it out. I rolled over and went back to sleep.

In the meantime, my parents were riding their bed across the floor. In hindsight, they should have thrown themselves from the unnaturally hyper piece of furniture and rushed out to rescue their children. In actual fact, they clung to the covers and sat frozen in fear, riding the world's only double-wide rodeo horse and watching their bunny slippers hop across the carpet in front of them.

The quake was over before you could say "Ride 'em cowboy"—earthquakes last forever when you're in the middle of them, but they always end before you can think—and Dad took his still-shaking self in to check on his children.

We were all sleeping soundly. This is because we were children, sweet and innocent in the belief that Mom and Dad could handle any situation without batting an eyelash. I personally do not actually believe that, but I can delude myself into anything if it means I get more sleep.

To Build a Fire

Carolyn

Several years ago, in the dead of a mild, yet chilly B.C. winter, our family gathered in front of the fireplace to relieve our poor shivering selves. We piled loads of sticks and newspaper into the fireplace, which was old and dirty. With great effort and the help of a good lighter, we finally got a small flame going.

Desperate to encourage the fire, we tossed the lighter aside and grabbed more newspaper. We hastily piled it atop the flames and watched happily as they blazed to life. In the mad shuffle to keep that small spark alive, the lighter was somehow buried under the newspaper. Into the fireplace it went with all the rest.

A large explosion sent us scurrying across the room at top speed. Mom sailed backwards, baby Andrew in her lap, at about eighty kilometers per hour.

All of this was harrowing, but not nearly as bad as the dark and stormy night in Port Coquitlam when our refrigerator held us all hostage. Without any warning, the fridge let off a loud explosion, accompanied by sparks. The entire household congregated around it, trying to figure out what was wrong. Our prognosis? We hadn't the faintest notion.

The fridge was in our laundry room, which was the central point of the house. Just the thought of a fire in our own Grand Central Station made a few of us consider sleeping outside. If only it hadn't been raining, we might have.

Dana woke sometime after midnight and heard the fridge explode again. She unlocked her lower bedroom window and yelled at her roommates, Sara and Elyssa. As they rolled out of bed, Dana ran across the hall and grabbed Andrew. With two crying little ones and a very sleepy Sara in tow, she exited the bedroom window and ran around to the side of the house, where she proceeded to ring the doorbell over and over again.

I woke to the sound of the doorbell and my mother yelling, "Fire! Get out of the house!" The six remaining pajama-clad Curreys ran into the laundry room, the site of both the Terror by Night and the side door. There, we found not a single tongue of fire. Our fears were for naught. Relieved, if not a little shaken, we trooped up to the living room and flopped on couches, blinking stupidly at each other.

The fridge never acted up again, and Dad eventually managed to fix it. But for some of us, the sound of a doorbell is still enough to spark our survival instincts—not unlike throwing a lighter into a fire.

Apocalyptic Wars of the Computer Age

Rachel

We Thomsons have been on the cutting edge of computerdom since the things were invented. Currently, we have a PC (Perpetual Catastrophe), which sits in our basement groaning like a card-carrying member of the computer tubercular asylum. It keeps me awake at night, both with its strange noises (reminiscent of one Jacob Marley) and with its ever-present threat of impending doom. Our whole life is dependent on that machine, which, as far as we can tell, is dependent only on the whims of its inscrutable nature to keep it going.

If our computer was an employee, we would have sent it packing years ago. It is not an employee. It is the boss. It tells us what to do, where to go, when to sleep, and how to live. We follow its commands like ants slaving for the Queen Mother. The computer is, after all, supposed to make life simpler. I protest that it does not do any such thing, but thus far, no member of my family believes me. (The exception to this is my mother, who has for years threatened to put an axe through the monitor.) My hypothesis is that the computer is a drain on society, on our family, and on life in general. I can prove it, too.

For one thing, the machine has the audacity to get sick all the time. It catches more viruses than I can track. Our family prides itself on health. We have come through whooping cough, asthma, pneumonia, and scarlet fever, but we have come through victoriously. The computer has no such pride. It succumbs to every little infection that comes along, scrambling our lives for days or weeks until we can find a way to cure it.

The human occupants of our house haven't seen a doctor in years. The computer has a doctor who comes and tinkers and frowns, and pulls wires and plugs wires and frowns more, and bites his nails, and strips the computer down to its skivvies. He pokes it, prods it, reloads this and unloads that, and in the end he pronounces it cured (for now) and hands us a monstrous bill. IBM (his Imperial Brain-Boggling Majesty) is still laughing.

There's more. Not only does our computer habitually threaten to die, but while it's in prime working condition it plots against us. It is a part of that great American conspiracy called *entertainment*. The computer sucks in innocent victims with enticements like Minesweeper, FreeCell, and worst of all, Spider Solitaire.

Spider Solitaire is not a game for the faint of heart, nor for the short of time. In order to master it, one must spend a minimum of three lifetimes and eight years in purgatory staring at the computer's green screen, moving little images sneakily designed to look like playing cards with a little image sneakily designed to look like an arrow.

The only member of the family who has proved herself totally immune to the computer's seductive lures is my mother. This is because she lives in a literal world. She has yet to develop that faith in the unseen which enables one to trust that pressing the "Save" button will actually save something. This is also because she has twelve children, and thus is way too busy to give a rip if Spider Solitaire is ever conquered or not.

Despite holdouts like Mom, computers threaten more and more to take over the world. My Uncle Brian, a preacher, recently told me that he has forgotten how to preach without Power Point notes. One day the electricity will go out, and the sheep will be shepherdless. Language has already largely fallen to the power of computers. Go online if u don't b/leev me b/c it's the truth. There is little hope left now 4 ne of us.

If you've a Perpetual Catastrophe in your house, might I suggest that you take up farming? A life spent in the soil is infinitely more attractive than a life spent in serfdom to Windows. But if you, like us, are too far gone for that, then I can only say that I am very sorry for you. Perhaps one day we will meet while lugging our computers to Central Command for yet another upgrade, and there on the street you will smile sadly and I will smile back, and we will both understand.

There's Gonna Be a Floody, Floody

Rachel

I was babysitting with utmost calm and decorum one day when Jimmy bolted up the stairs yelling, "Leah says 'get-downstairs-right-now-there's-water-all-over-the-floor!'" I laid my head on the table and groaned, then popped up, bounded down the stairs, and landed rather wetly on a concrete floor covered in two inches of warm water. Water had puddled against one wall and was lapping at the green carpet on the laundry room floor, seeping up the sides of cardboard boxes, and squishing beneath my toes.

Leah, whose pajama pants were hiked up to her knees, had already discovered the source, as it were, of the Nile. The hot water heater was pouring water from a pipe which at one time was connected to a little rubber hose leading to the sump pump. The sump pump sat in the far corner of the room, dry as a desert. The little rubber hose was nowhere to be seen. The pipe which should have been connected to the missing appendage was merrily dumping its load directly on the floor.

Once again, it was war against the machine.

Leah grabbed a bucket and a mop and frantically began bailing. I hauled loads of soggy laundry, boxes of thrift store clothing, and empty canning jars out of the way.

A few frantic minutes of battle availed us nothing. I bolted upstairs, leaving perfect footprints on the wood. A quick phone call alerted Dad to the situation, and he promised to come to our aid. He was, however, stuck in traffic. It would be a good half hour before he would arrive.

Now, there are not many things one can actually do when a hot water heater is behaving thus inconveniently. Temper tantrums and panic attacks are, of course, options; but not very useful ones. Another option is to scoop up buckets of water, run like crazy to the back door, toss out the water, run back, and repeat the exercise. This is rather futile. The water continues to pour all over the floor, making one's actions an exercise in frustration.

Another option is to reach for the nearest handy-dandy miracle product and hope it will do everything the commercials said it would do, such as making one's family perfect, cooking dinner in thirty seconds, and finally implementing world peace—all while doing a better job cleaning up spills than paper towels ever did.

As it happens, this is exactly what Leah and I did. The handy-dandy miracle product is called a Shammy Cloth. When wet, it soaks up the equivalent of Hoover Dam in roughly the same amount of time it takes to get a two-year-old ready for bed. It works amazingly well, although I have yet to see it cook dinner or implement world peace. As for making one's family perfect—well, we're working on it, but a cloth isn't going to do the job!

I ran to the bathroom and knocked the hitherto unused Shammy cloths off the top shelf. They landed on my head (more heavily than paper towels, I might add). I whipped off the rubber band holding them together and bounded back downstairs.

By this time the deluge had slowed to a steady trickle, which gave us hope. Leah and I laid the Shammy cloths over pillowcase-sized areas on the saturated carpet. (I know it was saturated because when I stepped on it, water shot up between my toes and hit me in the face.) Then we stomped all over the cloths. They are supposed to soak up water all by themselves, without any help from wine-making-wannabes, but you can hardly expect us to have been patient enough to let them.

I learned a few things from this situation. One, floods are a good way to get exercise (up the stairs, down the stairs; up the stairs, down the stairs) and a bad way to clean the basement floor, as they pull piles of muck from strange corners and spread it all over the place. Two, hot water heaters should always be connected to little rubber hoses, which should always be connected to sump pumps. And three, this might not be a bad way to make a living. Leah and I are thinking about custom-ordering a Shammy cloth the size of the average basement. When customers are in direst need, we can arrive with the thing on our shoulders, unroll it, and stomp all over it. We've even invented a stomping-all-over-it-dance. We shimmy while we Shammy, you see.

Personally, I think it's a brilliant marketing idea, which just goes to show that brilliant ideas can pop up in the most unexpected places—but if you're prone to having them, perhaps you should wait till you dry off before you start placing ads.

Part Four:

According to Plan (B)

Alberta

In Which We Get Lost in the Scenery and Peer Past Construction

Rachel:

Andrew Currey has a habit of overusing the word "awesome." "This food is awesome." "That game was awesome." "My peanut butter sandwich yesterday was awesome, but I'd rather eat a mouse than choke down this asparagus."

Aunt Cathie corrects it by saying, "God, Niagara Falls, and the Rocky Mountains are awesome. Nothing else. Eat your asparagus."

I had never seen the Rockies before our trip west. As they appeared on the far horizon of the plains, I sat up straighter in my seat and fidgeted with excitement. Mom had often told me about the mountains and what a truly—well, awesome—sight they are. And we were headed right through Alberta's famous Banff National Park.

We began to worry as we drew close to the tollbooth. A giant sign proclaimed entrance to the park—with a price tag, of course. The admission rates were outrageous. There was a decent family rate, provided your family consisted of no more than two adults and four children.

"We're just driving through," Uncle Dave told the girl at the window.

"Do you plan to stop?" she asked.

"Well," he told her, "we thought we would stop for lunch or a bathroom break, but then we'll keep going."

"You can go to the bathroom if you only stop for five minutes," she said. "Any longer than that and you have to pay the rates."

Aunt Cathie leaned over. "Can't we please have fifteen?" she asked. "You try sending eleven people and two dogs through the bathroom in five minutes."

The girl nodded slowly. "I suppose you can," she said. "But no real stopping!"

We drove into the park, its towering splendour all around us. "Ok," Aunt Cathie said as we drove into the park. "Here's how it works. One crew goes to the bathroom while another crew eats lunch and another crew runs up the path to Lake Louise. Then we switch. If we each take five minutes, we're not exactly breaking the rules."

We found a parking lot close to Lake Louise. As Uncle Dave searched out a spot, we passengers leaned forward with our fingers on our seatbelt buttons and all eyes on the doors. Ready, set, bathroom break!

Carolyn:

We, the multitudes, poured from the van, charging madly in all directions. Dad headed up the first crew to the bathroom with several older girls, short-legged little ones trying to keep up. Others of us scarfed down cheese sandwiches as fast as my mom could unpack them. For once, Andrew was not reprimanded for his chipmunk imitation.

In record time, we were ready to switch groups. While the first group parked themselves back at the van and ate lunch, Dad headed down the path to the lake at the rate of an express train. Mom hurtled up to the bathroom with several more people in tow.

I was with the first group to visit Lake Louise. Upon arrival, we discovered that things had not been properly arranged for our viewing. No, no one had moved the mountains or drained the lake—but construction workers had unceremoniously scattered machinery all over the place. Between the lake and ourselves was the biggest construction fence I had ever seen. You'd think it was a precautionary measure in case the Loch Ness monster had migrated!

We tried to take pictures of the lake and mountains while cleverly cutting out the construction, but we didn't have much time to fiddle around as my dad (the human motorized scooter) hastily turned his crew back to van and lunch. By this time the second group was finished eating, so they all headed off to the lake while we started lunch.

A third group headed to the bathrooms with Mom. We ate quickly and then waited. And waited. And wandered and took pictures and waited. After nearly twenty minutes they were sighted, charging back to the van at full (if weary) speed. Our time limit was shot to pieces.

As it turned out, my mom (the human dysfunctional compass) had tried to take a new route back to the van. The self-appointed guides with her offered reams of opinions, but they got hopelessly lost anyway. By the time they found us again they had toured not only the bathrooms and the lake, but three other parking lots as well!

Lunch and the Currey family disappeared back into the van. We wormed our way out through a maze of gawking sightseers, inattentive campers and impatient vehicles. Yes, we went over our fifteen minutes, but it wasn't our fault. We got lost coming back from the bathroom. It could have happened to anyone.

Rachel:

My grandfather has a book on his shelf that talks about living a "Plan B life." We'd all like things to go according to our original plans, but they seldom do—and Plan B syndrome is only compounded by the dynamics of family life.

How many times in your life have you found yourself settling for Plan B? It rains on your wedding day. The homeschool curriculum you laid out for the year is chucked out the window in the first month and replaced by a crash course in home repairs, home cooking, or home caring for those in need. You go to see the Rocky Mountains, and you wind up touring parking lots because Lake Louise is under construction.

Plan B lives are full of choices. You can look down at the pavement and pout because you're spending the forty-five minutes you didn't have looking for a large white van serving cheese sandwiches, or stop a minute and look up at the mountains around you. Cry because your children didn't learn to split an atom in science class this year, or smile because they stopped to smell the flowers. Sometimes Plan B turns out better than what you had in mind, anyway.

If there is anything that life in my big, slightly-insane family has taught me, it's that happiness is not dependent on circumstances. Happiness is a heart attitude, cultivated by prayer and a desire to live life to its fullest—in whatever shape it comes.

Hup! Hup! Hup!

Rachel

Six o'clock a.m. A brilliant light invades the darkness of the basement cave where Becky and I sleep. Dad's voice pipes in: "The sun's up! Time is slipping through our fingers! We have a major project to develop, create, and finish today (I forgot to tell you a month ago when I agreed to do it), and you have to be ready to leave the house in fifteen minutes. Come on, out of bed! Hup, hup, hup!"

Our character is built by the way we react to people and situations. Scripture compares the molding of our souls to the work of a potter with his clay. (Have you ever seen a potter at work? The words *mash, mangle, smush, smoosh, manhandle,* and *knead* come to mind. So do the words *big family*.)

Automatic enrollment in Character School is one of the greatest advantages of life in a big family. I'm going to build character whether I like it or not, or else I'm going to fold up and become a dried, useless lump. So, *mash*, *mangle*, and the rest of it aside, I'll choose to learn my lessons.

Even writing an essay like this one can be an exercise in character building. I sit down at my computer, and immediately a million or so people (are we *sure* there are only twelve kids in my family?) invade my den.

"What are you doing?"

"Rachel, I'm hungry."

"Anna needs a diaper change."

"Now what are you doing?"

"Do you wanna see my scrape?"

"Can I have some chocolate?"

"Can I have an apple?"

"Can I go outside?"

"It's too cold outside. Can I come in?"

"Anna took her pants off and threw them out the window."

"Look at this weird stuff on the chocolate. Is that mold?"

"Are you still working on that project? Why aren't you finished yet?"

"Dad just called. He needs that project like *now*."

"I ate the chocolate and now I feel sick. I think that was mold."

"There's a turkey vulture flying over the house. Come see."

"It's not a turkey vulture, it's a hawk."

"Is not."

"Is too."

"Is not."

"Is too."

"Jon just fell off the top bunk, and now his head's bleeding and Tirzah's screaming and I still feel sick."

"Hurry up, I need the computer."

"*Now* are you done?"

"Can you think of a good sentence with the word 'federation' in it?"

Tales of the Heartily Homeschooled

"Jimmy says mold is poisonous. Is it poisonous? I feel sick."

"Come look at my room, but first, you need to know it's not my fault."

"Can I go back outside?"

"I want to come in now because I just saw a brontosaurus* by the creek."

"See my ladybug? I'm gonna name him George. I gave him a bath."

"Rach, I *really* need the computer. What's taking you so long?"

"Is it almost supper time?"

"George is dead."

"What are you doing?"

You can see that there is much potential for reactionary behaviour here. Will I run off, screaming something incoherent about not being able to work when I'm being asked to grieve for a ladybug? Will I nail my little brother with a graceless comment about dinosaurs being extinct, for heaven's sake, and would you kindly stop bothering me about them? Or will I react in love and patience, remembering that the Christ who lives in me put up with people every second of His life here—that He loved them, even? Even when they asked ridiculous questions, which they did with alarming frequency, He loved them.

(Really, it's very good of God to give us people. He loves them and He loves to bless us with them. The truth is, once I calm down, I even love the ridiculous questions. They keep me laughing for years. Stressful days may be the ultimate in character-building, but they've got their blessings.)

Character school continues late at night when Deborah bounces off the ceiling with a "Sproing!" of night-personness. By this time, the little ones are in bed, and the older ones get up a friendly wrestling-kicking-screeching match, in which the only illegal move is tickling and the law is frequently broken. Mom and I are usually trying to drink tea in the midst of this, but it's hard to keep tea in your cup and off your clothes when you find yourself in the middle of a hurricane with legs.

What with meals, chores, emergency projects, dinosaurs and turkey vultures in the yard, morning people and night people, life in my house is a training course par excellence. I should be a saint in no time.

* For all you academic purists out there, I realize there is no way that my brother could have seen a brontosaurus by the creek. I calmly explained this to him. There was never any such thing as a brontosaurus. The skeleton given that name turned out to be a conglomeration of two other dinosaur species. I suspect the archaeologist responsible for the mix-up was trying to ward off a zillion questions while inserting Leg A into Socket B.

Taxi!

Carolyn

Ah, schedules. How easy they make life feel—until the schedule meets reality and results in something like a four-car pileup. One bright morning, I was scheduled to teach dance classes in Chilliwack while my teacher was away. I'd originally planned to get there half an hour early to turn on the heat and set up. A good schedule, no?

Disaster ensued the moment we stepped out of the house. When Mom turned the key in the ignition, all our big white van did was make a clickety-click sound. No matter how long and how creatively we pleaded with it, nothing would convince that engine to come alive.

We climbed out of the van. I stood in the driveway with my schedule fast unraveling. I had to teach a class in forty-five minutes at a studio twenty minutes away, and the van absolutely would *not* start. Furthermore, no one else could take over the classes. I didn't even have the other teachers' phone numbers. I was in a foul predicament.

(I do confess, however, that as these horrifying events unfolded, a little impish voice at the back of my head was chuckling, "Boy, this is funny. What an email this is going to make for Rachel!")

In vain I checked the phone book for a bus that would get me there on time. Finally I picked up the phone and dialed a taxi. Breathless, I waited for someone to answer my call and save the day. The ringing ceased—someone had picked up! But once again, my hopes, newly formulated as they were, seemed foiled. All I could hear on the other end was static.

In desperation, I suggested to my mother that I should perhaps start running, even though I probably wouldn't get there until next week. I would at least be on my way. I tried calling the taxi again and—oh, blessed sound—I picked out the faintest hint of a voice amidst the static. I finally heard the driver telling me to wait until he got around the mountain so he could hear me.

I couldn't wait until he got around the mountain. I hollered out my message, asked how much it would cost, choked at the price (for some reason *that* came through loud and clear), and listened to him say he'd be there in five minutes. Five minutes was optimistic, but he got there and hurried me to the studio with ten minutes to spare.

It was the first time in my life I had ever been in a taxi. It had the most awful gadget at the front that showed how much the ride was costing me as we went along. To my horror I calculated that it was going up at least ten cents every four seconds! The grand total came to more than half my day's wages. Misery me.

Once I got to the studio, I checked to make sure all of the CDs for the classes had been left for me. Shock No. Two for the day: the Grade 3 CD was not there. I ransacked the place, disrupting another class in my search for it, and finally learned that a student had taken it home with her.

The only thing that actually went according to schedule that day was my arrival home sometime before midnight. I looked at my shot-to-pieces schedule and rolled my eyes. I perused my schedule for the next day and rolled them again. What are the odds this one will go according to plan?

Papa Was a Gypsy, Mama Was a Rock

Rachel

I walked upstairs and stumbled upon a typical scene. It was April, and around our Michigan home a few inches of snow still lay on the ground. The skies were grey and the road was muddy. The temperature was far below decency.

We had been cooped up all winter, and it was beginning to show.

I entered the living room where Jimmy and Micaiah were rolling around on the floor in a tangle, wrestling. Micaiah was laughing so hard that it hurt just to look at her. On the couch, Keturah and Tirzah were sitting with their arms around each other. Keturah was sick with a bad ear infection and a fever. She and Tirzah, who heretofore had been perfectly healthy, were sharing a sucker.

Tales of the Heartily Homeschooled

I watched helplessly as it popped in and out of their mouths, spreading infection like plague-on-a-stick. In and out: Tuey's mouth, Tirzah's mouth. Anna crawled up on the couch to get in on the action.

Naomi shattered all of our eardrums with a bellow in the kitchen. Becky turned on a CD and began to dance around the living room, tripping over Jimmy and Micaiah. Jonathan marched in with a large piece of paper attached to his arm, announcing, "I've got a shield! Hey, Mom, look! I've got a shield! Look!"

Just then Keturah tangled the sucker in her hair. We fell to the task of removing it, while the noise level steadily grew and more people flooded into the room with problems and occupations of their own.

Dad walked in, looked upon this scene of pandemonium, and decided that it would be a good idea to coop the chaos inside a van and go on a road trip.

It happens every year. The scent of faraway lands rides in on the chilly April breeze, and we are stricken with travel fever. We long for nights spent with our chins resting on our knees, doubled up in a cramped vehicle. We yearn for the feeling of hundreds of miles of pavement passing away beneath our wheels. We begin to taste and smell the beef jerky and salami sandwiches. Most of all we desire to see things—mountains, oceans, greenery. Anything but the status quo.

Before long, we find some excuse to leave our home state and get the wheels of our fifteen-passenger van rolling. Other people take vacations; we do not. We take business trips. All of us.

We make lists, pack, dawdle, rush, pack some more, delay, forget some important things and lose others, and shuffle children from one place to another. At last, twelve or so hours after our planned departure time, we pull out of the driveway and head for distant horizons.

Our family's favourite destination is "south." It doesn't particularly matter where, but it should be someplace where they serve sausage gravy for breakfast and talk slower'n a possum crossing the street.

There are a lot of good reasons to go south. For one thing, it's warm. For another thing, there are mountains. And to top it all off, a trip south passes through a great deal of farm country, and thus it provides our family with the most important sort of scenery.

We drive along at a mind-numbing pace until an older child suddenly spots a bovine herd out one window. The scout leaps from her place like a kangaroo and shouts,

"Cows out Mom's window!"

This creates a flurry of activity as every seat explodes with questions.

"Where?"

"What cows?"

"Should I wake Anna up?"

"No!"

"Too late. She's awake."

The cows are soon behind us, and the van is left buzzing with adrenaline. Excitement dwindles down into whines.

"I'm hungry."

"The baby's stinky."

"Can I have a drink?"

Salami and bread are passed around along with a bottle

of water, diapers are changed, and everyone settles back in for the long ride. The calm lasts until a new scout leaps up and hollers, "Sheep on Dad's side!"

Once we reach the Appalachians, the scenery morphs: from farm animals and flatlands to high cliffs and purple lightning storms.

The craziest trip we have ever taken was embarked on while we were living in California. Dad booked our children's show, Dynamite the Dinosaur and Friends, in festivals all across the country. We took off in a borrowed 42-foot motor home for three months. It wasn't exactly the finding of the Northwest Passage, but it was a journey fraught with peril nonetheless. Here is the story of that epic trip, as I told it, via email, to Carolyn.

The Great Motor Home Adventure, Part One

Dear Carolyn,

About two—three? four?—years ago, Dad got it into his head to take us on tour all over the country. He booked

Dynamite the Dinosaur in festivals from California to West Virginia to Wisconsin. We had a lot of land to go see! We acquired a motor home and added a little trailer on the back of it to carry our equipment (our giant inflatable stage set and costumes), and off we went!

Well, first we dawdled at home for a day too long, and *then* off we went! As a result, we were late for our first show, which was in Tennessee. We only had a few short days to get there. We tore through the desert with wild abandon, forgoing sleep and peace of mind in a mad race to reach Itchycoo. (I kid you not—that was the name of the festival.)

Did you know that riding in a motor home is a lot like riding in a boat? You have to get your sea legs. We were all sick and lying about the place moaning and groaning within the first half hour on the road. When you walk in a moving motor home (especially if Dad's driving), you basically get around by clinging to something, aiming yourself at something else, and then letting go so that the motion of the vehicle pitches you in the right direction. We got pretty good at all of this, except poor Mom, who could hardly move the whole trip. Oh yes, and when you go on a motor home trip, make sure you take things like full tea kettles off the counter before you get going. Otherwise they will slide off and drop on your big toe (Injury No. One of the Great Motor Home Adventure, sustained, naturally, by me).

After a long day's drive, we all tried to settle in for the night. We stretched out on the bed, table, floor, couch—anywhere there was room. The ride was bumpy and uncomfortable, but we succeeded in drifting off to sleep.

That is, all except Mom and Dad, who were staring in shock and dismay at the "check engine" light. The motor home was new to us, so they didn't want to take any chances. Far off on the Arizona horizon they could see a gas station, but how to reach it? Where was the exit to take them off the freeway to find aid? They spotted a small road that seemed to wind in the direction of the station, so they pulled off.

I slowly came to consciousness as the world bumped and rattled quite dreadfully around us. Possibly it was the mirror falling off the wall and shattering all over the floor that clued me in? I don't remember . . . in any case, I was aware that we were quite lost and that Mom and Dad were quietly fuming in the front seat.

I drifted off again, willing myself to believe that we were really on the road to Tennessee and all the lostness was a bad dream, but soon I realized that we had stopped. I emitted a groan, knowing instinctively what was to come. A moment later Dad bellowed from outside, "Honey, tell the girls to get up and put pants on! I need help out here!"

Groggily, we arose from our places of repose, pulled shorts and pants on underneath our nightgowns, and filed dutifully outside. We were in the desert. Very much in the desert. In a very . . . deserted desert.

Apparently, Dad had decided to turn the motor home around when the road dead-ended in a dry creek bed full of enormous boulders. He had driven out into the desert, down a slight decline, turned around, and failed to get the trailer back onto the road. It was disconnected while the motor home was hauled back on course, and now it sat smugly at the foot of a small incline, containing five hundred pounds worth of equipment and just daring us to budge it.

We put our shoulders to the grindstone (or is that "noses to the wheel?") and pushed and pulled with all our might, until at last we did get the trailer up onto the road. In the process, I sustained Injury No. Two: a pinched nerve that acted up for the rest of the trip and got so bad I couldn't walk at times. As we tried to hook the trailer back up to the motor home, Dad dropped it on his foot—Injury No. Three.

So that you will not be kept in suspense, I will assure you that we did indeed make it to Itchycoo Park on time, though when we got there, no one knew who on earth we were or what we wanted. It was the most disorganized event I have ever seen, and someone finally figured out where we were supposed to go when they found a program that had been dropped in the mud.

I shall end this installment of the Great Motor Home Adventure with those lovely words, "To be continued . . ."

Talk to you later!
Love,
Rachel

Tales of the Heartily Homeschooled

The Great Motor Home Adventure, Part Two

In the last installment I related the injuries which we sustained on our persons, but said nothing of the injuries which the (borrowed) vehicle incurred. My fingers are numb and near to falling off because it is very cold in this basement where I type, but I shall try to tell the tale before I sign off.

At Itchycoo Park, we drove our motor home to a stage in the middle of a great, barren plain. Far, far away in the distance, the rest of the festival could be seen. I do believe I mentioned that this event was poorly planned, so the only witnesses to our show were those few brave souls who trekked the miles, with their children in wagons and strollers, in search of the children's stage. We performed three times a day to small crowds; small in stature, years, and quantity.

Then, suddenly, our stage was mobbed by teenage girls. No, I must admit, they had not come because they wanted to see us sing and dance around in dinosaur costumes. A teen heartthrob act just happened to be on right after us, and they'd all come early to get good seats on the grass. We made all the girls quite green with envy, as we were allowed backstage and they weren't, but we weren't much interested in meeting the heartthrobs, who all had long girlish hair and squeaky voices. And that great crowd had to sit through one of our performances! It just so happens that we videotaped that one. The girls were told that they would be on TV, so they were very enthusiastic, and on the video you can see them mobbing the stage.

We left Tennessee in a blaze of glory. We decided to try our first campground—hitherto we had been spending nights in Wal-Mart parking lots. We pulled in, and Dad got out to hook up the water and electricity. In the meantime, we made ourselves comfortable, pulling the curtain all the way around the windshield.

A moment later Dad reentered, explaining that the van had to be pulled further back. Accordingly, he unveiled one half of the windshield and backed up for all he was worth. A loud smacking noise alerted us that something was wrong.

We unveiled the other half of the window to discover that the side-view mirror had hit a tree and was now dangling from a wire.

Later, in West Virginia, we dropped Mom and Deborah off at a laundromat while the rest of us attempted to go grocery shopping. All of us kids threw ourselves onto the bed at the back of the motor home and shouted directions at Dad while he backed the van up. It sounded something like this:

"Keep going . . . keep going . . . no, turn left!"

"You mean right, Rachel."

"Oh, right. Right!"

"You're doing good . . . No, that's a little too far . . ."

"Dad! The trailer's going to hit a—"

Crunch.

The finished sentence would have been, "The trailer's going to hit a minivan with a grouchy owner who is watching us from the door of the laundromat!" Later that day, after things had been settled with the minivan driver, we drove over a railroad track so fast that all of the cushions flew off of the bed and came down in various areas of the bedroom. My neck and back took a long time to recover.

I shall go now before my fingers fall off. A hot cup of tea that I forgot about hours ago (which I suppose makes it a cold cup of tea) is waiting for me in the microwave.

Coming up in The Great Motor Home Adventure Part Three: Asthmatics, Italians, and Little Bitty Windy Streets.

Talk to you later!
Love,
Rachel

The Great Motor Home Adventure, Part Three

After a long delay, here is the last installment of the Great Motor Home Adventure. After Itchycoo, we headed for Clarksburg, West Virginia, where I promptly caught cold and came down with a bout of asthma. We were scheduled to perform three times a day for three days at the Italian Heritage Festival. As I am sure you are aware, there is not a speck of Italian blood in our veins, so how we ever ended up marching our blue-eyed, blonde-haired way into a celebration of garlic, tomatoes, and Mediterranean culture I will never fully understand. We did have one thing resoundingly in common with many of the Italians, however: our large family. Out of all the festivals we played on that trip, we had the most fun at that one.

Of course, I was rather miserable, as it's hard to sing "In the Jungle" three times a day when you are rasping, coughing, and blowing your nose every five seconds. Somehow I survived, and even, for the most part, managed to recover.

One of the acts that used the stage after us was an Italian Dance Troupe. You would have loved to see it. They did Italian and Gypsy folk dances, and the members of the troupe ranged in age from four to seventy-eight. They had everyone in the crowd come and join in on a few songs. We danced too; it was great fun.

On the last day of the Italian festival, we headed out in search of a quality Italian restaurant we'd been told to try. Let it be noted that Clarksburg is built on the side of a mountain, and its streets are narrow and windy. Let it also be noted that our motor home was anything but windable. That thing bends like a ramrod.

After getting stuck in the festival parking lot and blocking traffic for fifteen minutes, we headed up the mountain, rounded a corner, and heard a sickening crunch as the side of the motor home closely encountered a telephone pole. This caused more blocked traffic and more damage to the motor home. (Not to mention our pride! It's hard to be inconspicuous when you're blocking a whole street in a vehicle the size of a blimp.)

After West Virginia, we headed north and west for Wisconsin, where we played at a Christian festival and slept in a 150-year-old church.

At long last, we headed back to California. We made one more stop in Arkansas to look at a property. We went roaming across acres of woods and grassland, where we got a flat tire. Dad fixed it while being eaten alive by ticks. He came down with Lyme's disease on account of that, and God healed him later, but that's another story for another time.

Tales of the Heartily Homeschooled

Thus endeth the Great Motor Home Adventure. We all came out alive, which is a mercy, although we no longer have the motor home. We'd have to be crazy to do it again—which probably means we will someday.

Love,
Rachel

Charge of the Apple Brigade

Carolyn

When we moved into our house in Agassiz, British Columbia, our explorations of the yard quickly yielded an apple tree. Visions of pies, crisps, and other delights danced through our heads. The apple blossoms budded and bloomed, and we dutifully prevented the little ones from making bouquets. The fruit grew larger as the summer waned, until patience ceased to be a virtue and we made our first raids on the tree. We reveled in fresh apples for several weeks. But as autumn approached, the apples ceased to look fresh. Mom gave the official order: "Pick them all, and leave not a sproutling on the tree."

We swarmed the tree on ladders and branches, removing the fruit at only slight risk to our necks. Fallen apples were gathered and sorted into buckets labeled "Good," "Bruised," and "Very Bruised." Armed with peeling and chopping knives, cutting boards and garbage pails, we prepared to make a mass charge on the harvest. Every single apple had to be hand-peeled, chopped small, and stored in the freezer for future use.

On the surface, it must have been a picturesque sight: five sisters peeling apples under a tree in late summer. But things are never as they look on the surface. We soon ran into an unexpected problem. Worms.

Many of the apples, it turned out, had residents. Christa proclaimed her passionate loathing of the creatures and refused to come into contact with any apple that might house one. That wasn't going to work too well, as it meant she couldn't touch any of the apples. Convenient for her, maybe; but she wasn't going to wriggle out of work that easily. Finally we came to an agreement: I would cut each apple in half and check for worms before she cut it up.

It was a good system for a while, although every time a worm was found Christa made disgusted faces and inched away from it. We settled into a routine. I peeled for dear life, quickly stopped to halve Christa's apple, and returned to my former job. We worked for hours and acquired very quick peeling skills (along with sore fingers). All went well until I started going a little too fast, and I didn't notice that an apple I handed to Christa was inhabited. It was purely accidental, I assure you!

It didn't take long for Christa to find not one but two worms in the apple. She hurled it across the yard and took off shrieking. It took a group effort of reasoning, ordering, and manhandling to convince her to pick up another apple. After that, every time a worm was sighted, she took off like a torpedo.

Once our fingers were blistered, we decided to quit for the day. We made resolutions to finish on the morrow as we trudged back to the house bearing our harvest. Actually, we never went back to the apples. For the rest of the summer, one last bucket rotted on our deck while we studiously ignored it. Our raw fingers eventually healed, and we can eat apples again—but to this day the mere mention of a worm is enough to make Christa wrinkle her nose and back away fast!

Clutter Wars

Rachel

My friend Michelle once declared that when she grew up she was going to be a minimalist. After a recent move, she called me up to lament that she and her husband have more stuff between the two of them than my entire family of fourteen.

Snicker if you wish, but this state of affairs is hardly Michelle's fault. She spent a number of years teaching and still more in ministry, and so for years she received far more than her share of holiday and special-event teddy bears, candle holders, plaques, and gingko-eucalyptus shampoo and conditioner. Things only got worse when she got married, and she struggled to raise her head above the aftermath of three showers as well as the actual wedding presents themselves.

For a good while, whenever the subject of Michelle's stuff came up, I was content to murmur sympathetically and secretly gloat that I had escaped such a fate. However, lately I am not so quick to smirk. One corner of my bedroom is beginning to burgeon with things that are good for nothing but reminding me in a very graphic manner how much I really need to dust. (Things are getting out of hand when my snow globe looks like the Oklahoma Dust Bowl.)

There are a few reasons for this foreboding pile of things, one being the year I spent teaching preschool, another being the few years I spent in ministry. But there is a greater culprit. I have yet to discover how to avoid it, for every year it bears down on me unrelentingly. I am speaking of my birthday.

My birthday was three days ago, and as I write this, my pile of birthday presents is springing up before my very eyes. Every morning I am awakened by two sweet little faces peering into mine as their hands pat the covers under which I repose. When I open my eyes, a present, wrapped in a suspiciously familiar piece of purple wrapping paper and taped within an inch of its life, is thrust into my face.

This morning I was given a small stuffed rabbit with one ear slit open, "for to sleep with," as Tirzah said. Yesterday I acquired a broken plastic doll house, and this afternoon I obtained a large pink Barbie-shoe key chain.

What to do with these things I don't know. I certainly don't have anywhere to put them. I plan to try the usual tactic: I'll keep the presents at the foot of my bed until a reasonable length of time has passed and then sneak them back up to the little girls' room in hopes that they will have forgotten all about giving them to me.

The worst part is that these toys don't really belong to the kids. They belong to the Thrift Store.

Mind you, we don't *have* a Thrift Store, at least not in the brick-and-mortar sense of the word. What we have is inventory: two years worth of outgrown clothing, dog-eared paperbacks, and 10-gallon garbage bags overflowing with old stuffed animals. A few years back, we tried to empty our house of clutter. We had garbage bags and banana boxes piled up by the front door, just waiting to be given the bum's rush, when Dad looked up, jumped up, and exclaimed, "What are you doing? We need all that for the Thrift Store!"

In that moment, the Thomson Gift & Thrift was born. That store is like death and taxes—it'll be with us always. It has stayed faithfully by our side, in our storage locker, piled in our basement, and arrayed throughout our living room through six moves. It blocked our hallways in Novi and provided a nesting place for mice in our garage in Saline.

We have a dream: that someday, the Thrift Store will move to an actual thrift store, and we will be rid of its abundant treasures at last. So far, though, not one measly shoe or stuffed monster has made it onto a shelf. Instead of shrinking, our pile of clutter continues to grow like a man-eating weed.

Someday, I fancy, the Thrift Store will force us out of our home. "Rachel," my parents will say, "it's time for you to be off and married. We need your room to store galoshes."

Room by room, the Thrift Store will eat up our house

until all that's left is the kitchen and the bathrooms. Those of my siblings who are too young to go off and marry will end up sleeping on top of the fridge and doing their schoolwork in the bathtub. The smallest children, I imagine, will wander off through the maze of clutter in search of new toys, every day straying further and further until they cannot make it back again. One by one, the Thrift Store will swallow my family into oblivion. It's a harrowing prospect.

If I had a choice about it, I would add my voice to Michelle's. I want to be a minimalist when I grow up. Take my advice—stay away from bargain bins and resale shops. When someone offers you something, say, "No, thank you, I think we have one of those already," even if it's a 3500-year-old Egyptian sarcophagus. Clean out your closet once a year, and give away anything you don't wear anymore. Clutter may seem like a small problem to you, but once it gets out of hand, it will quickly pass the point of no return. Stay away from stuff.

But if you're looking for a pink Barbie-shoe key chain, I think I have one available.

Faith, Trust, and Windshield Wiper Fluid

Rachel

When it came to driving, I was a late bloomer. For years I lacked that intense desire to legally roll a vehicle over pavement which possesses so many teenagers. I was eighteen before I got my permit.

I took a few behind-the-wheel lessons from a Driver's Ed teacher, and then I was left to face the real test of courage: driving with my parents.

There is something demeaning to teenage pride about seeing your mother's fingernail marks in the dashboard to the right of you. Likewise, no young, independent spirit takes kindly to having her father lunge across and grab the steering wheel when once she strays, an *itsy-bitsy bit*, too far toward the car on the left.

My parents and I were in Birch Run, Michigan, one night, about an hour and a half from home. Time was swiftly trickling toward permit expiration, and I was not yet competent enough to take a driver's test. So I volunteered to drive home.

Did I forget to mention that Dad had decided to take a shortcut?

As we blundered down a sharply winding dirt road in the darkness, my relationship with my parents suffered strain. My mother sat in the front seat with her hands over her eyes. My father, who had been falling asleep at the wheel only half an hour before, sat in the back giving contradictory instructions and further agitating my mother.

I bore down on the brakes as a sign ahead pointed to a curve. The van crawled through the curve.

"You don't have to slow down when there's no change in the speed limit," Dad said.

Another curve was just ahead, and I still couldn't see the road. I flew through the bend, and Mom grabbed the armrest.

Dad made a noise in the backseat, and Mom said, "You told her not to slow down."

"Unless she can't see the road," he argued.

"I couldn't see the road *last* time," I said. "That's why I slowed down."

I made a left turn at Dad's instruction. "Now keep going," he said. "We'll take this road all the way home."

Twenty minutes later, we were faced with another dead end. I turned left.

"Do you know where we are now?" I asked.

"No. No idea. Keep going."

It started to rain, and I turned on the wipers too soon and too slow. They promptly smeared the windshield beyond all sensible standards of vision just as we hit another curve.

"Should I use the fluid stuff?" I asked.

"I think we're out of fluid stuff," Mom answered.

"Turn the wipers on faster!" Dad said.

This story does have a happy ending. I figured out how to use the wipers, and the windshield defogged. The dirt road we were on turned into familiar territory. Dad never went back to sleep, but then, Mom didn't have a heart attack either.

It seems to me now that careening down that unfamiliar road in the middle of the night was a bit like taking a new path in life. Take homeschooling, for instance. Many years ago, Dad sat me on his lap and said, very seriously, "You're not going to school anymore." I was a reluctant kindergartner at the time, so that was okay with me! But as I've gotten older, I've realized that homeschooling is a vehicle on a sometimes uncertain path. Dad doesn't always know where we're going. Mom isn't always comfortable with the bumps in the road. And me? Well, I count myself blessed if I can successfully navigate the next turn, much less hang on to "the big picture."

We all have tools to get us through each day: schedules, skills, subjects. But more important than the trappings of a homeschooling life are the gifts God gives us, which we have to choose to make use of. Patience. Trust. Love.

On the road that night, our relational skills were strained. We snapped at each other as outward stress got worse.

In doing so, we missed the point—that only by working together could we get home. When life becomes an exercise in frustration, it can be important to sit back and realize that we have all we really need in each other. Close your eyes and remember how much you love your family. Determine to put your trust in God. Pray for patience. You *will* reach the end of the road!

Next time I'm on the road with my parents—be it Highway 69 or the daily winding road of life—I intend to make liberal use of faith and trust. Oh, and windshield wiper fluid isn't a bad idea either.

Let It Rain

Rachel

Some creation scientists theorize that it never rained on the earth before Noah's Flood. They figure mists came up from the ground and watered everything. That must have made Noah's threats interesting, to say the least. "Repent, or it will water upside down! Really!" Nowadays, of course, rain is a significant part of life.

The word "rain" brings a whole list of other words to my mind. Thunder. Spring. Moving.

You may question the inclusion of that last word, but take my word for it—it belongs there. You see, there is a scientifically provable link between Thomson family moves and rain. We move, it rains. It's infallible, as relentless as gravity. You doubt it?

We moved to the Mojave Desert. It rains only one and one half times a year in the Mojave Desert. It rained.

We moved out of the Mojave Desert. It rained again.

We moved to Michigan in January, after weeks upon weeks of snow. It rained.

We moved to a new house in Michigan after a two-month drought that threatened to topple the agricultural workings of the Midwest. It thundered four seconds after we lowered the ramp on the moving truck. As soon as we carried the first box from the house to the truck, it rained. It did not let up until after we'd finished moving into the new place.

I've looked at this issue backwards, forwards, and inside out, and I hereby relinquish it to someone smarter than myself. Could you please explain? What is it about the sight of Thomsons hauling cardboard boxes that makes the skies pour forth? I do have one explanation: God has a sense of humour. I tell people this and they look at me strangely, but I defy anyone else to come up with something better!

At this point, we're considering hiring ourselves out. Any community in desperate need of water is welcome to pay us large amounts of money to move in. Hiring us is easier than digging wells and doesn't look as silly as performing a rain dance. We'll stay until the deluge lets up and then be on our way again—which means they'll get two downpours for the price of one.

When I moved cross-country with the Curreys, it only rained when we were safely indoors. This has me greatly relieved, because it means that I do not personally act as a traveling rain magnet. I was beginning to worry. Just imagine if my future husband had the same malady. What could we expect when we moved? Hurricanes? Earthquakes? Blood and fire?

I have to admit I felt a bit lost during the Currey move. I'm unused to moving furniture without splashing through puddles. The sight of a moving truck or an empty house is strange to me without water on my glasses to make the scene blurry. Once or twice, when I got very thirsty, I tipped my head back and opened my mouth, and nothing happened. It was very disconcerting.

My family is currently packing up for another move, this time over the border into Canada. We're stocking up on rain ponchos and galoshes. We figure an international move deserves something extra special from up above. If we're really fortunate, maybe we won't even have to drive. We'll just stick our arms out the windows of the van and paddle.

Canning Peaches the (Nearly) Painless Way
Carolyn

As I write, I have just finished canning eight cans of peaches. It remains to be seen whether the seals will take or not, but we hope for the best. I gleaned a few worthy notes from today's instructional activity. Should you ever decide to embark on the terrifying and perilous chore of canning, study them. May they serve you well.

First of all, amusement is always necessary when embarking on a task like this. Be creative, and you'll find entertainment in all sorts of convenient places. I discovered that when you roll a large slice of peach in freshly made peach jam and suddenly pop the whole thing into Christa's mouth, she will make a noise of mingled horror and delight, classified between a squawk and a squeal. The side effect of jam dripping down her chin was most enjoyable to observe.

The flippant side of things quickly faded for me, though. I felt my eyebrows begin to draw firmly together. My breath grew laboured as I felt myself sucked into a vortex of unfamiliar jars, sealed lids, and complete sanitization.

If you, like me, are not already familiar with the number of jars needed, the quantities of peaches and syrup necessary, etc, you may run into a slight discrepancy. This may result in a mad look that will spring into your eyes as you shove and squash peaches into jars, declaring, "I *will* fit in these last two peaches!" And odds are, you will.

When you place full jars in a large pot of water, said pot may spill over due to water displacement. This may cause all the gas elements on the stove to flood and go out.

If you do not clean up the ensuing spill (because you didn't see it and it was under a large pot of water—not because you're naturally negligent), but you turn the gas on again anyway, the stove will emit a dreadful stench. You may not notice that you are in danger of dying from gas fumes because you're flying around like a mad woman cleaning up the disaster. Fortunately, your mother will probably notice and rush in to save your life.

You may add to the flurry of a boil-over disaster by noticing flames that are rising high and not responding when you switch off the dial. You should then yell at all the little kids in range, "Go find your mother and tell her that the *stove is on fire!*" They will run off and spread the message. In the meantime, you will discover that you turned off the wrong dial, and nothing is wrong after all. Now, however, you have instituted mass panic, which you will need to quench.

Yes, canning for the first time is certainly an interesting endeavour. Despite nearly burning the house down, flooding the stove, half choking myself, and causing household hysteria, I think I did pretty well. There are now six jars of peaches steaming on the counter, and I believe they're all sealing. Except for one. Maybe if I jam a few more peaches in, reboil the jar, use a bit of glue on the lid . . .

Salvation in the Mailbox

Rachel

I check our mailbox, oh, two or three times a day. It's a compulsive habit. Every time I go outside, be it seven in the morning or twelve at night, I walk down the driveway and open the box, as though I think there will be something in it. I know perfectly well that nothing will be there. Tirzah runs out the front door every day at two o'clock (which is when the mail comes) and brings the mail into the house. Usually there is nothing for me, just some fliers, bills, and free magazines.

I think this is why I keep checking the box: because there *should* be something for me. Some old friend should have sent me a letter, or a present, or maybe some money. Money would be nice. I think I keep checking the post because someday something is going to come that will solve all of our financial problems. I am waiting for salvation in the mailbox.

I've always looked for salvation in unexpected places. If I found myself in a strange place when I was younger, I would half-anticipate that a big group of my friends or relatives would suddenly show up and rescue me. They rarely did show up, so I had to learn to stand on my own two feet a bit, and I suppose this was good for me. And there have been times over the years when I was hungry; usually when we were away from home for the day and we didn't have money for food, so we'd eat when we got home.

In this situation I always waited for someone—anyone—to take a sudden liking to us and offer to buy us dinner. You can imagine how often *that* happened. People don't generally carry enough money on them to feed a family of our proportions. Even back in the old days we were large enough to give would-be benefactors pause. But even today, nothing pleases me more than being taken out to eat. Maybe I see it as vindication of all those years of hoping.

In literary terms, this sort of "salvation in the mailbox" is known as *deus ex machina:* "god from the machine." I think it refers to old Greek plays in which the hero would be trapped in an utterly hopeless situation, only to be rescued in an unexpected way by a god who was lowered to the stage by a crane.

I've used *deus ex machina* in my novels. I can't help it. The ancient Greeks probably checked their mailboxes twenty times a day. So do I, and so do my characters, and I can't keep letting them down when the box proves empty.

Yesterday I checked the mailbox when I left for my walk at eight o'clock in the evening, and I checked it again when I returned at nine. That's when all of this hit me: all of this "salvation" business. But I think I'll keep checking the mailbox, if for no other reason than to remind myself that I have a Biblical mandate to believe in the impossible.

1 Corinthians 13:7 commands me to "bear all things, believe all things, hope all things, endure all things."

Victor Hugo said it very nicely:

> "Hope, child, to-morrow, and to-morrow still,
> And every morrow hope; trust while you live.
> Hope! each time the dawn doth heaven fill,
> Be there to ask as God is there to give."

My hope isn't silly, and it isn't futile. There really is a God working in my life who comes through at unexpected times and in unexpected ways. I think I have an advantage over those who look for help only in logical ways. My life is exciting. I never know what will happen tomorrow, but I know that God will be in it.

And do you know something? I think I get taken out to lunch more often than other people. I think that my friends show up where I don't expect them more often than they would under normal circumstances. Maybe I'm wrong, and other people experience these things as much or more than I do. But I enjoy them more, because I've been looking for them.

Others may pound the pulpit of reason and logic and shout from the rooftops that miracles do not happen, but I plan to keep on checking for salvation in the mailbox.

We're Jesus's People

Rachel

I was babysitting one day, and the house was in a rare state of quiet. Tirzah was curled up in the big armchair by the window, golden strands of hair falling across her face. Her forehead was creased slightly as she studied the picture book on her lap and did her six-year-old best to read the words to herself.

I noticed Keturah entering the room with little paper people taped to her fingertips. They had beards and tiny hats: priests or Pharisees, perhaps, carefully traced from a Bible story colouring book.

Keturah and her paper men slipped around the back of the chair where Tirzah was sitting. A moment later the paper men popped up over the back of the chair and Keturah's five-year-old voice chirped, "Hello! We're Jesus's people! We've come to tell you about Jesus!"

I'm not sure where Keturah learned the art of evangelism, but I know where she learned who Jesus is. I learned the same way: from my family. After my grandmother died, my aunt wrote me a note telling me about the day I was born. Grandma was holding me for the first time, and she glowed at me and said, "Jesus loves you."

Those are some of the first words a child in our family hears. They are soon followed by other words: "God made you. Jesus died for you. Did you know that Jesus never did anything wrong? He died for the bad things *we* do, so we can go to Heaven with Him. If you ever need anything you should ask God for it. Do you know how big God is? Bigger than this house! Bigger than the sky! God made the earth and moon and sun and stars, and He is bigger than the whole universe!"

With every lesson comes the growing knowledge that these are the things *we* believe, the truths that distinguish us. We're different from the world. We are Jesus's people.

I grew up watching not only my parents, but also my grandparents, aunts, uncles, cousins, and family friends who made the same claim. As I grew, I matched words with actions and learned what it really meant to be one of Jesus's people. We don't lie, steal, or slander, because Jesus would not want us to do those things. We don't have twelve kids by accident—we have them because God said they were blessings, and we want all the blessings He will give us. We homeschool because we believe God asked us to do it. We eat good food instead of junk food because God made good food, and we believe He knew what He was doing. Everything relates back to Him.

Parents who claim to be Jesus's people need to be aware that their actions either confirm their words or battle against them. Eventually, children who grew up singing "Jesus Loves Me" will begin to recognize things in the lives of their elders which do not harmonize with being people of God. There's a chance that these children will write their parents off as hypocrites and reject what they've been taught all their lives.

Then again, they might do what I did. (And this is made so much easier by parents who strive to practice what they preach while admitting their failures, confessing their sins, and humbling themselves before God and others.) They may come to realize that being one of Jesus's people is about being a weak sinner surrendered to God's strong grace.

The fact that my family members are imperfect and still follow God is actually an encouragement. It means there's nothing stopping me from following Him, too. My failures don't keep me from being a child of God any more than they keep me from being a Thomson.

Somewhere in all those lessons, between "Noah built the ark" and "God so loved the world," is "You can't get to heaven on your mother's apron strings." Eventually, those of us who grew up in Christian homes have to make the choice for ourselves, to define ourselves by belief in God or not.

I made the choice to follow Jesus when I was six. I've re-made that choice several times since then. Carolyn recently wrote to tell me that Elyssa, four years old at the time, had gone leaping through the house after everyone had gone to bed, jumping on beds and proclaiming, "Wakey, wakey, I'm a Christian!" Jonathan committed his life to God a few years ago, and now, at the age of eight, is the family's chief theological student and corrector. ("Did you know" and "That's not true" are two of his favorite phrases.)

The Christian life is a journey marked by many milestones. Through the advancing years of dedications, first prayers, conversions, baptisms, and re-dedications, it's nice to know that we're not alone. We're part of God's family, all of us Jesus's people, learning and growing together.

These days it's not uncommon for someone to ask me if there is some special religion behind our family. (Other than the twelve kids, long-haired girls, polite boys, respectful attitudes, and modest clothing, I can't think why they would ask.) I usually just smile and say, "Yes: we're Christians." No special category, just Christians. Just Jesus's people, out in the world, different and trying to make a difference.

Like most things, that difference starts at home.

Did You Enjoy This Book?

Do you know someone who would enjoy reading it? SPREAD THE WORD! As a small press, we value the power of READERS to decide what is worth reading. We believe that a book's true value cannot be measured in marketing dollars. The worth of a book is in the impact it has on YOU. If you have seen value in this book, we encourage you to let others know.

It's simple:

- Spread the word!

- Give a copy as a gift.

- Leave a review on Amazon.com or BarnesandNoble.com. Then email us a copy so we can post it on LittleDozen.com.

- If you write a newsletter, ezine, blog, or print column, consider letting your readers know about this book!

- Send us an email: publisher@littledozen.com

Visit the authors at
http://rachelstarrthomson.blogspot.com

Free Fiction from Little Dozen Press

Worlds Unseen

Book 1 of the Seventh World Trilogy

by Rachel Starr Thomson

FREE to Download from www.LittleDozen.com
Also Available for Purchase in Softcover Form

A fantasy adventure, *Worlds Unseen* follows the journey of Maggie Sheffield as she searches for truth in a world bound by darkness and deception. Along with the Gifted gypsy Nicolas Fisher, who hears things no one else can, Maggie joins with the last surviving members of the Council for Exploration Into Worlds Unseen and a group of easterners led by a ploughman and a princess as they rebel against the forces of the Blackness.

"I fell in love with Worlds Unseen. I finished it a few moments ago, with tears in my eyes. It was really touching…and brilliant, and beautiful. The whole thing reminded me of a mix between C.S. Lewis, Ted Dekker, and Diana Wynne Jones, while being wholly different."

"Your story is wonderful! You are such an artist and you paint such beautiful metaphors. I am in awe."

"You have a gorgeous poetic way of putting things that's incredible and enviable. I love the huge grand scale of things that your world runs on, yet your characters make it personal in such an amazing way."

Coming Soon from Little Dozen Press

Burning Light

Book 2 of The Seventh World Trilogy

The further adventures of Nicolas Fisher, Maggie Sheffield, and a cast of new characters as they stand against waking evil and prepare the way for the King.

As the world takes sides, their lives play an integral role: in the coming of light, or the triumph of darkness.

Coming to Paperback December 2008.

For more information, visit
www.LittleDozen.com

Devotional Writing from Little Dozen Press

Heart to Heart:
Meeting With God in the Lord's Prayer

by Rachel Starr Thomson

Read Excerpts or Purchase at www.LittleDozen.com

"Father." With a single word, Jesus Christ ushered His disciples into a new relationship with their Creator. With a single prayer, He opened a door into the heart of God. In this highly engaging and personal work, Rachel Starr Thomson takes readers on a journey through the most powerful prayer of all time—straight to the heart of the Father.

"This book is not merely a job well done, though it is that; it is truly a significant contribution to the devotional literature on the Lord's Prayer. I thought it was one of the best things on the Lord's Prayer I have read—a true devotional experience based on Jesus' prayer." - Michael Phillips, bestselling author of *God: A Good Father* and The Stonewycke Legacy

"Phrase by phrase, sometimes word by word, the author moves through the Lord's Prayer ... The book begins in the Garden of Eden, touches on the lives of familiar figures in the Bible, and calls us to make an honest evaluation of our own lives and walk with God. This is a book I'll return to, the next time life gets over-busy and my prayers seem dry and profitless. *Heart to Heart* is a drink of cool, refreshing water in a parched and thirsty land." - Jean Hall, Eclectic Homeschool Online (www.eho.org)

"I will never again view this simple but powerful prayer in the same light."
- Crystal Paine, BiblicalWomanhood.com

Devotional Writing from Little Dozen Press

Letters to a Samuel Generation: The Collection

by Rachel Starr Thomson

FREE to Read at www.LittleDozen.com
Also Available for Purchase in Hardcover

This collection of essays was originally published as a devotional ezine. Now available as a hardbound book from Little Dozen Press, *Letters* has encouraged believers all over the world, from teenagers and missionaries to mothers and pastors.

"I have really appreciated your *Letters to a Samuel Generation*. It's been a blessing to be able to include them in our publications to inspire our younger (and older) readers. I appreciate how you are able to keep a balance in building faith, yet acknowledging pain. Calling to action, yet reminding people that BEing comes out of doing. And calling for unity, while still stressing the need to stand for truth." - Mercy Hope, regular columnist for *An Encouraging Word* Magazine, and interviewer for FaithTalks.com

"I recently read your article entitled 'Beauty' in the Home School Digest magazine. As my mom commented, the writing and message were 'beautiful.' I found it very encouraging that people exist who realize the departure of true Godly beauty from our arts, society, and lives. It also inspired me to be one who, with God's strength, shines to the world HIS beauty." - Aaron Dodson, age 19

"Just a note to say that I really enjoyed this month's ezine . . . to your description of what God's practical love is, my spirit shouted a resounding 'yes!'" - Robin Gilman, homeschooling mother of 10

www.ingramcontent.com/pod-product-compliance
Lightning Source LLC
Chambersburg PA
CBHW031245290426
44109CB00012B/444